Love, Honor, and Finances

Building Oneness in Marriage

Ray Lynch

ISBN: 978-0-9708399-2-3

CONTENTS

ACKNOWLEDGMENTS

I would like to express my gratitude and appreciation to all those who made the completion of this book possible.

To God for being longsuffering with me, redeeming me, empowering me, gifting me, entrusting me with my wife, Judy, and giving me two wonderful children, Casey and Erin.

To my loving wife and best friend, Judy, who loves God and is obedient to His Word and has been a blessing to my life.

To Terry and John Harris, my sister and my brother-in-law, who apart from my wife are my greatest encouragers.

To Dennis Kestler, Chris and Lora Weihe, Dan and Tina Stumpfhauser, and Deanna Stephens for the many hours they devoted to the review of the manuscript and for their insightful comments that helped to improve the book.

To Kelly Nielsen, who created the book's cover, and to his wife, Teresa, who came up with the title of the book.

To the many contributors to LifeChange Concepts who over the years have given sacrificially so that I could be one of the few full-time Christian financial stewardship/budgeting counselors in the United States.

To those who currently serve on the LifeChange Concepts Board of Directors and those past Directors who have given of their time and talents and have wisely directed the ministry over the years.

To the pastors and teachers who have correctly taught me the Word of God over the past twenty-five years, which has not only allowed me to grow in the grace and knowledge of Jesus Christ, but has equipped me to write this book.

To Evan Braun and Word Alive Press, whose professional editing helped me clarify the message of this book.

To Rick Dillman, Mahlon Hetrick, and Henry Bieber who God used in my life to grow me professionally.

INTRODUCTION

Amazing grace how sweet the sound, that saved a wretch like me...
—*John Newton*

I first thought about writing *Love, Honor, and Finances* while I was teaching in the Engaged Couples Class at Idlewild Baptist Church in Tampa, Florida. As I would look over the couples in each class, so happy and so in love, I would remember the many couples I had already counseled through LifeChange Concepts whose marriages had fallen apart, in many cases as a result of finances, and I would think, *These folks don't have a clue as to what they are in for.*

In the four hours I had to give them a glimpse into biblical financial stewardship, I would try to give them ideas for cultivating oneness in their marriages through finances. I would merge together the wonderful truths of God's Word with the day-to-day responsibilities and challenges of personal finances in a way that would hopefully enable them to build strong marriages. Strong marriages and strong financial stewardship complement each other. You seldom see one without the other. Finances encompass every aspect of our lives. If we cannot create oneness in our finances, it will be very difficult to do so in our marriage relationships.

The Apostle Paul wrote in 1 Corinthians 15:9 that he was *"the least of the apostles"* (NIV). Paul knew that his history of persecuting Christians made him unworthy of even being called an apostle. I can relate to Paul's feelings of unworthiness. I am the last person who should be writing a book on marriage relations. Like Paul, my history regarding marriage is poor. The marriage I will refer to often in this book is actually my third marriage. Even though my first two marriages occurred before I trusted Jesus for the forgiveness of my sins and understood the importance of having Him as the foundation of my life and marriage, it is still difficult for me to have two failed marriages on my resume.

Like Paul, I hurt many people by being a poor husband and walking away from these two relationships. Prior to writing this book, few people knew I had been married three times. Most thought I had been married only once before. In my flesh, I would prefer to keep it this way. However, I share this painful part of my life for the sole purpose of magnifying my Lord and Savior, Jesus Christ. I stand in awe of His grace, which not only allowed me a third try at marriage, but was and is the sole reason for the success of my current marriage.

When I repented of my sins and put my trust in Jesus for forgiveness on November 29, 1986, I made a commitment to God that I would live my life by His principles and commands as found in the Bible. Whether it was being a husband to my wife or a father to my children, whether at work or with our finances, I pledged to do it God's way. Although I still sin, my heart's desire is to present my body as a living and holy sacrifice, acceptable to God every day of my life. Through God's grace, my wife and I have a great marriage. In *Love, Honor, and Finances*, I will share not only what God says about money, but also aspects of our marriage and finances in order to help you build oneness in your marriage through the way you manage the resources entrusted to you by God.

The truth is that many marriages are failing. Many of these divorces find their roots in the chaos and disagreements of family finances. The problem has nothing to do with having too much money or too little. There are great marriages amongst couples with little means as well as amongst those with an abundance of wealth. Conversely, some couples have poor marriages regardless of their socioeconomic state. So what causes two people who love each other deeply and cannot stand to be apart from each other when they first meet to reach a point where they are not even friends and have little or no positive things to say about each other? Every year, I counsel couples that have reached this point or are on the road to it. What causes this? For many, it is their inability to incorporate God's principles, particularly those for money, into their marriage and lives.

Each counselee coming to LifeChange Concepts must complete an intake questionnaire. Through their responses to the questionnaire and during the counseling sessions, we find out how couples handle their finances. The following are typical answers we receive:

- We communicate very little with regards to financial decisions.

- We disagree on many financial issues and fight often.

- My spouse handles all the finances and, apart from some big financial decisions, they do not include me.

- We are not living on a written budget and our spending is out of control.

- We have separate checking accounts and split the bills.

- My spouse buys things for himself/herself without consulting me, so I retaliate by buying things for myself, resulting in a continual "buying war."

- I pay the bills and my husband is not involved in the finances except to complain if a bill is not paid on time.

- If there is money in the checking account, we generally do what we want at the time.

- We use credit cards for emergency situations, because we have little or no savings.

- My husband/wife pays the bills and lets me know when I must stop spending.

- We pay all our bills on time, but our credit card balances are rising.

- The only time we discuss the finances is when there is a crisis.

Each of the above methods of handling finances as a couple has one thing in common: they are all *oneness inhibiters*. In this book, I share the biblical approach to managing your finances which creates *oneness enhancers*.

Divorce and unhappy marriages were not God's plan when He created man and woman. Having parents that divorced when I was fifteen years old, and then having my first two marriages end in divorce, has given me a better understanding of why God said He hates divorce—*"For I hate divorce,' says the Lord, the God of Israel"* (Malachi 2:16). The world tells us that it is better for the children that we divorce rather than letting them have to live with parents who don't like each other. The world also recommends divorce because we each deserve to have happy marriages, and our current spouse surely isn't the right one.

I bought into these lies and regret it deeply. Many people today are also buying into these lies. If you are thinking about divorce, are unhappy with your marriage, or just want to elevate your good marriage to a great marriage, my prayer would be that you would read this book with an open and teachable heart and that you allow God to change you and the way you relate with your spouse over finances and other aspects of your life.

God wants oneness for your marriage. With the consummation of the first marriage between Adam and Eve, God's Word says, *"For this reason a man shall leave his father and mother, and be joined to his wife; and they shall become one flesh"* (Genesis 2:24). He didn't put you and your spouse together so that you could go through life as two unhappy, independent people living under one roof—nor did He put you together only to have you divorce. He wants you to have a great marriage!

The sad truth is that I haven't met a single couple that didn't want to have a great marriage, and yet the divorce rate is at an all-time high. In Chapter One, I will tell you why God wants us to have great marriages, and throughout the book I will be transparent about my own marriage and share biblical principles and disciplines to help you achieve one.

If God could take a twice-divorced man and create oneness in his marriage, He can do the same for you. In reading this book, you will learn that my wife and I are not perfect people, and yet, by God's power, we can have a super marriage. So, open your hearts to God and allow Him to speak to you through this book.

5

Ray Lynch

CHAPTER ONE:
ONENESS

But I have this against you, that you have left your first love.

Revelation 2:4

My First Love

This isn't just a book about budgeting and numbers, because biblical financial stewardship is about so much more than that. At the time of this writing, I have been doing one-on-one Christian financial counseling for twenty-two years. I was saved at the age of thirty-nine, back in November 1986 when Pastor Karl Skinner of Battlefield Baptist Church in Gainesville, Virginia shared the good news of the death, burial, and resurrection of Jesus.

Because of my business and finance background, I began to study what the Bible said about money. For the first ten years my focus as a financial/budget counselor was on the numbers. This is what I was comfortable with. Things were more black and white to me during that period regarding giving, saving, and spending. I taught what the Bible said about the ways we use God's money, but it was still primarily about the numbers.

Then, about eleven years ago, God gently revealed to me that it wasn't just about the numbers. In truth, it's about love. The very first of the Ten Commandments was, *"You shall have no other gods before Me"* (Exodus 20:3). God dearly wants to have a relationship with us. Indeed, God paid a stiff price in order for us to have that relationship: His one and only Son, Jesus, had to die on a cross. In order to begin this relationship, you must first do what I did on that November 29, 1986 evening: understand that you are a sinner in need of a Savior, and by faith put your trust in Jesus for the forgiveness of your sins (see Ephesians 2:8–9, Romans 3:23, Romans 6:23, and Romans 10:9). If you have already put your trust in Jesus, I congratulate you on making the most important decision of your life. If you haven't, I encourage you to do so today.

Even though people come to LifeChange Concepts (LCC) for financial counseling, God occasionally directs unsaved individuals and couples to us. Such was the case with Larry and Connie in 2005. During our second session together, the Holy Spirit prompted me to stop the financial counseling and ask them, "If you died tonight, where would you spend eternity?" Each gave a works response, meaning that they believed their good works would get them to heaven. After showing them the above scriptures, they both prayed to trust Jesus alone for the forgiveness of their sins.

At our third session, Connie came with a Bible. She had already read the four gospels. The positive way they were interacting with each other stood in stark contrast to our first two sessions, before they'd accepted the gift of salvation. Immediately after praying to start the session, Connie shared how she had been planning to contact a divorce attorney before coming to LCC, but now she readily admitted that she was a major source of unhappiness in their relationship. Her newfound humility was the opposite of her earlier blame-game approach.

God makes salvation so easy that even a child can understand it, which this counseling experience demonstrated. However, though many today have made Jesus their Savior, they have not all allowed Him to be Lord of their lives. Five years later, I can say that Larry and Connie have a great marriage, even though they've actually been through more financial difficulties than before they came to LCC. This is because they made Jesus Lord of their marriage.

Money and possessions are part of our lives, but for many they represent too great a part. Jesus said, in His Sermon on the Mount, *"No one can serve two masters; for either he will hate the one and love the other, or he will be devoted to one and despise the other. You cannot serve God and wealth"* (Matthew 6:24). Jesus was telling us that it is humanly impossible to love God and money at the same time. James stated it clearly when he wrote, *"Therefore whoever wishes to be a friend of the world makes himself an enemy of God"* (James 4:4).

Money and possessions distract us from trusting and loving God in a way that He desires. God wants to be preeminent in our lives. Number one! In *The Fourth Frontier*, author Stephan Graves puts it this way:

> *Many followers of Christ, if asked to list their priorities, would order them this way: God, family, self, and work. The fact is an integrated holistic view of life includes work. Consider a new set of priorities for life: God. That's it. There is no number two or number three or number four. In living out a commitment to that priority, we must make Him an integrated part of everything we do—family, self, and work.*[1]

---

[1] Graves, Stephen R. *The Fourth Frontier* (Nashville, TN: Word Publishing, 2000), p. 9.

To that, I would add finances, which encompasses all of life.

Many Christians put God in some, but not all, of the compartments of their lives. For instance, they might say, "He can be in my Sunday morning worship compartment, or my Bible study compartment, but He doesn't need to be in my car shopping compartment or my job compartment."

Jesus said it this way: *"But seek first His kingdom and His righteousness, and all these things will be added to you"* (Matthew 6:33). God wants to be intimately involved in every part of our lives, including our money and possessions. Near the end of his life, Moses spoke to the people of Israel a song of praise and adoration to the Lord, and then he said to them, *"Take to your heart all the words with which I am warning you today, which you shall command your sons to observe carefully, even all the words of this law. For it is not an idle word for you; indeed it is your life"* (Deuteronomy 32:46–47). The Bible is not an idle word to be pulled out only on Sunday mornings; it is to be our life. The Word of God should be lived out in every part of our life, but most certainly our finances.

No particular amount of money and possessions is responsible for distracting us from loving God with all our heart, soul, mind, and strength. The Bible is full of stories of people who had great wealth; some loved God deeply while others did not. Conversely, there are examples in the Bible of people with very little wealth, some of whom loved God while others did not.

This book does speak to the practical skills of budgeting, but it is really about building oneness with God. How you manage the resources entrusted to you by God will either move you closer to that oneness or further away.

My Other, Earthly Love

Since this book is written primarily for couples, I will assume that you have found a second love: your spouse. Unfortunately, many who read this book are doing so because their marriage is in trouble, particularly in the area of finances. Their second love has become their worst nightmare. For some, this book may be enough to begin the healing process. But for many, marriage counseling with a Christian counselor will be necessary in order to deal with deeper issues. If this is the case with you, seek out a godly counselor to help you.

Just as God desires us to be in oneness with Him, He also desires for us to be in oneness with our spouse. In bringing Adam and Eve together God said, *"For this reason a man shall leave his father and mother, and be joined to his wife; and they shall become one flesh"* (Genesis 2:24). You'll be less likely to achieve oneness in both your finances and your marriage if either of your parents is still involved financially and emotionally. If you (the wife) run back to mother every time you have a disagreement with your husband, you have not left "your father and mother." If you (the husband) run back to your parents for financial help every time you hit a bump in the road, you have not left "your father and mother." There are times when you may need your parents' help (abuse, serious financial hardship, providing financial help to allow the wife to stay at home with the children, etc.) but an ongoing emotional and financial attachment is not healthy, particularly when your parents use the attachments to control you. I'm not telling you to never talk to your parents again, but God wants you to create your own culture—a culture of oneness, where you are dependent on Him first, then each other, and then, if God permits, temporary help from others.

Oneness in marriage is so important to God because of what marriage represents. Marriage is an earthly picture of the marriage between Christ and the church (i.e. the body of believers) that will occur when Jesus returns to get His bride. God wants our earthly marriage to be like our heavenly marriage. Oneness means having a deep love for each other.

Finances are a deterrent to a great marriage, as many surveys attest. Money is the number one reason for marital conflict. It is believed that seventy percent of failed marriages in America fail over finances. But that was not God's plan, and the fact that we are still sinners after salvation hasn't caught God off-guard, either. He knows that money has an emotional component that, when coupled with our sin nature, creates control, power, love, guilt, and many other struggles.

I am not a licensed therapist and therefore will not delve into these psychological issues, but I will discuss our differences regarding money and possessions, and how you can turn them into good, rather than evil. That is *always* God's plan. Joseph understood the sovereignty of God and the goodness of God and, as a result, was able to tell his brothers, who had sold him into slavery, *"Do not be afraid, for am I in God's place? As for you, you meant evil against me, but God meant it for good in order to bring about this present result, to preserve many people alive"* (Genesis 50:19–20).

God is sovereign, in control, and His plan is for good—not for evil. It doesn't matter where you are in your marriage relationship—whether you feel that you have hit bottom or are fast approaching it—God wants to preserve your marriage. In the next chapter, I will discuss our beliefs about money and how they can create good rather than evil. If you have a good marriage or are just starting out in your marriage, my prayer is that this book will give you the tools to not only achieve God's financial goals, but to build a great marriage.

> **Key Point: Building oneness with God will help you build oneness with your spouse.**

Cultivating Oneness Out of God's Love

If you focus on imitating Jesus Christ, oneness in your finances will begin to occur. Take some time with your spouse to discuss the following questions:

1. Are you managing the resources God has entrusted to you for His glory or for your gratification? What areas of your life are you not allowing Him to be Lord over?

2. What are you doing to promote oneness in your finances?

3. What are you doing to hinder oneness in your finances?

4. Have you separated financially and emotionally to a healthy level from your parents? If not, discuss with your spouse how you can change that.

Have you put your trust in Jesus for the forgiveness of your sins (and for eternal life)? If not, I encourage you to do so today. Call LifeChange Concepts at 813-244-7042 if you want to know how you can have eternal life.

We have been married for over thirty-seven years. From the very first day of our marriage, our monies have been combined into a single joint account. We both have agreed that no matter what the source (job salaries, inheritance, etc.) the funds would go into our joint account. Also, when it came to donations, we've agreed to distribute available monies to various Christ-centered ministries, which is one way we have found to give back to our Lord and Savior for the many blessings He has bestowed upon us.

—Larry and Jeanie Bailey
San Antonio, TX

CHAPTER TWO:
GETTING TO KNOW
EACH OTHER AND GOD

And do not be conformed to this world, but be transformed
by the renewing of your mind, so that you may prove what the
will of God is, that which is good and acceptable and perfect.
Romans 12:2

Money Beliefs: What Are They and Where Do They Come From?

Someone once said, "Before marriage opposites attract, and during marriage they attack!" Why is it that the very qualities that attract us to another person end up being irreconcilable differences in divorce court?

First, let me say that I believe that opposites being attracted to each other is not a coincidence; it's a God thing. C.S. Lewis believed that the devil constantly tries to trick us to extremes." God's Word says, *"But each one is tempted when, by his own evil desire, he is dragged away and enticed. Then, after desire has conceived, it gives birth to sin; and sin, when it is full-grown, gives birth to death"* (James 1:14–15, NIV).

What Lewis and James were saying is that, left to ourselves, our sin natures could gravitate towards extreme behavior. For example, my parents drummed into me as a child the importance of spending less money than I earned. Their teaching of the importance of saving, combined with my God-given frugal personality, resulted in me always being a saver. In my second marriage, my saver's bent prevented me from achieving balance between saving and spending, and therefore I failed to meet my spouse's emotional needs. She pulled away from me and I didn't have a clue why. If I had taken the time to understand her needs, God could have used that understanding to bring my saving and spending desires into conformity with His will. However, since God was neither Lord of my second marriage nor my life, I clung to my saving beliefs and our marriage failed.

One of the ways in which we are often different from our spouses is in how we think about money. In her book *For Richer, Not Poorer*, Ruth Hayden calls these attitudes "money beliefs." We all have them, and as Ruth says in her book, "They control your money behaviors."[2] She goes on to say that these "beliefs are an internalized emotional response to a life experience."[3] When our money beliefs conflict with those of our spouse (and they often will, because opposites attract), we begin to have problems.

In her book, Ruth has a number of practical exercises couples can use to help them identify their money beliefs, understand the emotions tied to them, and communicate and create real, lasting change in their money lives. Although I cover some of the same ideas, I don't examine them to the same depth that Ruth does in

---

[2] Hayden, Ruth L. *For Richer, Not Poorer* (Deerfield Beach, FL: Health Communication, 1999), p. 47.
[3] Ibid., p. 52.

her book. Therefore, I recommend it as an additional resource for most couples reading this book.

In Chapter Seven, I discuss in more detail the common wrong attitudes we have about money and how they contrast godly attitudes.

The Story of Mike and Mary

Mike and Mary once came for counseling. A quick look at their financial status left me wondering why they had come to LifeChange Concepts at all. They were generous givers, active in their church, and diligent in their Bible studies.

However, as with about half of the couples I see, they were looking for someone to break the financial stalemate. They had about $35,000 in their emergency savings and Mike had a very good commission sales position. I urge families whose income fluctuates wildly, like Mike's did, to have six to twelve months of spending needs in savings, particularly when they are a single-income family like Mike and Mary were. Even though their savings met the lower range of this standard, Mary felt strongly that $35,000 was not enough. When most people, including Mike, would be rejoicing, why was Mary in fear of not having enough savings?

As Mary shared her financial history, I began to understand her fear. At age twelve, Mary's life took a significant turn for the worse. It was at this point in her life that her parents' business failed. They were committed Christians, and therefore believed that they should pay back all those who they owed. As a result, they decided to sell their home and move from their upper middleclass neighborhood to the government projects so they could slowly pay everyone back.

The guys reading this may not get it, but I have no doubt that every woman reading this has already figured out why Mary was so concerned with building a large savings account. When Mary got to this point in her story, she pointed her finger at me and said, in a very determined tone, "This will never happen to our daughter!" Moving away from her comfortable lifestyle and all of her friends at twelve years old had created a huge money belief that, twenty-one years later, was generating disagreement in her marriage.

Many of the money beliefs we have, like Mary's, cannot be supported by the teachings of the Bible. Although it is the heart of every parent to protect his or her children from harm, it is not in our power to do so completely. God is in control and He orchestrates our life's circumstances in a way that will mature us as believers and bring us closer to His image. This is called sanctification.

No amount of savings could guarantee that Mike and Mary's daughter would not experience the same thing that Mary did. Quite frankly, Mary turned out to be an awesome Christian wife and mother. James wrote, *"Consider it all joy, my brethren, when you encounter various trials, knowing that the testing of your faith produces endurance. And let endurance have its perfect result, so that you may be perfect and complete, lacking in nothing"* (James 1:2–4).

I am sure that Mary is a strong Christian today partly because of the uncompromising integrity modeled by her parents throughout her life, but also because of this trial, which took away her friends and comfortable lifestyle. Do we like going through trials? They aren't fun, but they do accomplish God's plan to mature us, if we handle them correctly. What parent wouldn't die to have his or her child turn out "perfect and complete, lacking in nothing?"

Exercise 4, at the end of the chapter, lists some financial money beliefs I have heard over my years of counseling. I encourage you to complete the exercise and see if it unearths any of your own money beliefs. The exercise does not cover all possibilities, so it will be important for you to sit down with your spouse and share your stories with each other, particularly as they relate to finances. As you hear your partner's story, you will begin to understand why they are the way they are with money, and you will have empathy.

In Chapters Seven and Ten through Fourteen, I will discuss many of God's principles on money. You will be able to compare your emotion-driven money beliefs with the truth of God's Word. This will be a key to you creating oneness in your finances.

So, let's look at the good news.

Good News

Since this book is about building oneness in our marriage, let me close this chapter with the good news about opposites attracting. Someone once said, "Differences create conflict, and conflict can be the catalyst for intimacy." Your marriage will either move towards intimate oneness or away from it by the way you view your differences. If you view your spouse's money beliefs as nothing more than a hindrance to you getting what you want, your marriage will not experience intimacy and you will not grow more Christ-like. On the other hand, if you see their money beliefs and the stories behind them as something delicious that needs to be pursued and understood, your marriage will grow stronger and you will be more conformed into the image of Christ.

The conflict that arises from differing opinions exposes our sinful attitudes and beliefs, and if we deal with our sins as God exposes them, we will have great relationships with our spouses and God. However, a word of warning: Don't preach to your spouse about his or her sinful attitudes like I did with Judy early in our marriage. This only created more discord. Instead, allow God to speak to his or her heart. Be patient, understanding that what may be obvious to us may not be to your spouse.

In the case of Mike and Mary, Mike moved towards his wife's need for more savings (which is not a bad thing), while Mary, after seeing the conflict between her money belief and God's Word, began to move towards Mike's position on savings. The end result was that they were closer to oneness in their finances and relationship, and probably closer to where God wanted them to be financially.

Shortly after being born again, my Sunday school teacher shared the following diagram with me. It is a perfect picture of what God wants in our marriages: overcoming our differences by focusing our eyes on Christ. As we conform more to the will of God, we will find ourselves drawing closer to our mate.

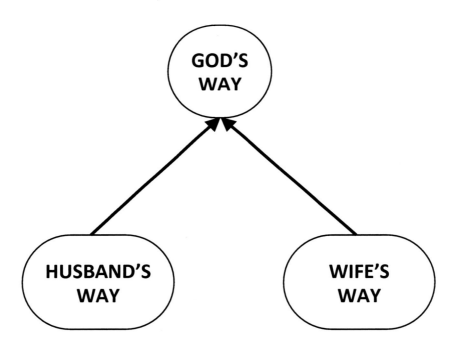

Not that I have already obtained it or have already become perfect, but I press on so that I may lay hold of that for which also I was laid hold of by Christ Jesus. Brethren, I do not regard myself as having laid hold of it yet; but one thing I do: forgetting what lies behind and reaching forward to what lies ahead, I press on toward the goal for the prize of the upward call of God in Christ Jesus. Let us therefore, as many as are perfect, have this attitude; and if in anything you have a different attitude, God will reveal that also to you; however, let us keep living by the same standard to which we have attained. Brethren, join in following my example, and observe those who walk according to the pattern you have in us. For many walk, of whom I often told you, and now tell you even weeping, that they are enemies of the cross of Christ, whose end is destruction, whose god is their appetite, and whose glory is in their shame, who set their minds on earthly things. For our citizenship is in heaven, from which also we eagerly wait for a Savior, the Lord Jesus Christ; who will transform the body of our humble state into conformity with the body of His glory, by the exertion of the power that He has even to subject all things to Himself.

Philippians 3:12–21

Key Point: God wants to use the differences between you and your spouse to draw you closer to Him and to each other.

Cultivating Oneness Out of Your Differences

Understand that God is using the differences in the way you and your spouse think about money to make you both into the image of Christ. The discomfort created by our differences should be resolved. By resolving our differences in a biblical manner, we grow more like Christ. By ignoring them, we remain apart from each other and God's will for each of us.

1. List the reasons you believe God put the two of you together. Don't rush through this exercise. Take time to remember.

2. Tell your spouse how his or her differences from you make you and your marriage stronger. Don't limit your answers to just finances. For instance, my wife processes decisions slowly, which helps to balance out my quick processing mind.

Use the following activities to get to know your spouse better:

1. Share with your spouse what it is about them that makes you feel secure or insecure about your family's financial future. The one that is listening cannot speak or defend himself or herself (see James 1:19–20, Ecclesiastes 3:7). As the listener, you should not judge your spouse's remarks, but you may ask questions to better identify what you can do to reduce the insecurity. For instance, your spouse may tell you that you make her feel insecure by not participating in the finances. A follow-up question

asking for specific things you could do that would lessen her insecurity would be appropriate.

2. Identify your money beliefs and try to determine the source(s) of these beliefs. How do you think your money beliefs compare to God's principles on money?

The following is a list of money beliefs. If any of these statements seem true and make sense to you, circle the number. If you have to think long and hard over a money belief, it is probably not one of yours. Do this individually and then discuss with your spouse. What are the emotions (pride, fear, selfishness, etc.) behind your money beliefs? What are the stories or experiences behind your money beliefs?

After you have identified your money beliefs, discuss how they may be causing strife in your marriage. For instance, one of you may have circled #18 while the other circled #19. Or maybe one of you is like #12 whereas the other is like #31. Do you see how conflict could arise out of these differences? How could these differences become a strength for you and your marriage?

1. There's never enough money—ever.

2. I am comfortable with very little in savings as long as I can pay my bills.

3. Money involves just one financial crisis after another.

4. I don't need to get my spouse's approval every time I buy something.

5. If I want something, I deserve to get it.

6. If I have money in my pocket, I will spend it.

7. I won't say no to my children, even when times are tough financially.

8. Our problems will work themselves out. We don't need to change what we are doing.

9. Why use your own money when you can use someone else's by borrowing.

10. Whoever earns the most money should have the bigger say about how the money is spent.

11. I could be successful with money if I wasn't married.

12. I rarely get what I want while others in my life get what they want.

13. People take advantage of me, and I let them.

14. I have a hard time having fun with money.

15. I feel like I need to hide how much money I have and not be showy.

16. I'm scared of trying to balance my checkbook.

17. I'm scared of paying bills. What if there's not enough? What if I need the money for something else that comes up?

18. No amount of money in the bank makes me feel safe.

19. I'm not disciplined enough to be good with money.

20. Picking up the bill for a meal with friends makes me feel important.

21. I have never been good with numbers.

22. God doesn't really care how we spend our money.

23. You need to take risks if you hope to succeed.

24. Men are supposed to take care of the family finances.

25. My income is my money.

26. I wish we/I could do more for our/my children.

27. Someone will bail me out.

28. Having nice things makes me feel successful.

29. If I could earn a little more money or have a bigger home, I would be content.

30. If I can make the payment on my debts, everything is fine.

31. Spending money makes me feel good.

32. My children deserve to have more than I had as a child.

Trust in the Lord with all your heart and do not lean on **your own understanding**. *In all your ways acknowledge Him, and He will make your paths straight.*
                                   Proverbs 3:5–6, emphasis added

Additional Resources
For Richer, Not Poorer, by Ruth Hayden.

We are passionate about trusting God with our money, but it wasn't always easy. We tried various ways to keep our finances under control, but consistently failed. Our marriage was strained due to money talk dominated by fears and insecurities. Even in our attempts to stay afloat, we were still slowly drifting apart.

Through a series of events, which included a friend giving us Ray Lynch's first finance book, Budgeting for the Non-Accountant, *God brought us to an understanding of the meaning of true financial freedom. At this point, we were determined to live on a budget. We set out to create some financial guidelines, which gave us a forum to share our needs, priorities, dreams, and goals. Living on a budget fosters communication in our marriage, thereby building trust and intimacy. We are now partners walking in financial oneness as we focus on our long-term goals.*

—Mike and Erin Jackman
Haymarket, Virginia

CHAPTER THREE:
LOVE, HONOR, AND FINANCES

But godliness actually is a means of great gain when accompanied by contentment.

1 Timothy 6:6

Marriages in Jeopardy

Bob and Anne arrive for their first financial counseling session and appear to have a mixture of anger and indifference towards each other. There is little or no energy between them. They have been married nineteen years and have two children. They both work and pay their bills on time, but the stress of living paycheck to paycheck has taken a toll on their marriage

Approximately twenty-five percent of married couples that have come to LifeChange Concepts for financial counsel arrive, like Bob and Anne, with their marriage very much in jeopardy. Many of these couples have been married more than fifteen years, but instead of having a deep love for each other (as God wants) they aren't even friends. As I sit and observe these couples who now dislike each other, I wonder what took place to drive them so far apart. The love they once had for each other in the early years of their marriage vanished, leaving them to just go through the motions.

While counseling a middle-aged married couple, Jack and Martha, in 2003, God revealed to me one way in which the improper handling of family finances can cause a marriage to die. In our first session together, Martha shared her financial history, starting with her high school days of working after school to earn money to buy clothes and concluding with their present situation. As she shared about how stressful her current job was, she suddenly began to pound on the table while almost screaming, "I need a vacation," over and over again.

Before each counseling session, I ask the Holy Spirit to guide me. At that moment, I was glad that the Holy Spirit was with me. Quite frankly, I don't know how I would have responded without the Spirit's intervention. After Martha settled down, the room grew quiet and the Spirit prompted me to ask Jack how her request made him feel. His response was quick and to the point. He said that it made him feel inadequate and insignificant.

Jack felt inadequate and insignificant because he knew that they did not have the financial resources to satisfy his wife's desire for a vacation. Quite simply put, he felt that he was not providing for his wife's needs.

Martha didn't intend to make Jack feel insignificant, but she was doing a great job of it. This financial issue—of not being able to afford a vacation—was having a significant impact on their relationship. However, it was not the lack of a vacation that was the problem.

After the session, I took some time to reflect on what had just transpired. God began to reveal to me truths from His Word that would help this marriage, as well as many others. In the remainder of this chapter, I will tell you what God shared with me.

Men and Women Are Different

As you probably already know, men and women are wired differently. God created most men to have a greater heartfelt need for significance than women. On the other hand, women have a greater heartfelt need for security. In 2004, Dr. Emerson Eggerichs wrote a book called *Love & Respect*, in which he explained the connection between God's commands to husbands and wives and their emotional needs. In Ephesians 5:22 and 33, God commands wives to submit to their husbands as to the Lord and to respect or honor their husbands. By respecting and honoring her husband, a wife feeds her husband's need for significance.

In Ephesians 5:25, God commands husbands to love their wives, just as Christ loved the church, and to give themselves up for their wives. By loving his wife with unconditional and sacrificial love, a husband feeds his wife's need for security.

So what does all this have to do with finances? A great deal! Husbands and wives may be undermining the heartfelt needs of their spouse, just as Martha was, without even knowing it.

Helping Your Husband to Feel Significant

The first thing a wife must understand is that most husbands want to be good providers for their families. It is in our DNA. This is why God created most men to have such a strong emotional need for significance; this need drives a man to get a job and work hard. Work helps to fill this need, but it also provides for his family. Sadly, modern American society and the women's liberation movement have emasculated many men to the point that this God-given drive has been suppressed.

Two problems arise when this emotional need isn't balanced by the Word of God. First, some men fail to balance work with their family's other needs and end up destroying the very thing they are trying to make better. Secondly, men's desire to provide has driven them to allow their families to spend more than they can afford, resulting in large amounts of debt. Today's materialistic society has established lifestyle requirements and credit cards have provided the means to achieve them.

Even though these problems exist, however, the truth is that men need to work and want to provide for their families.

Let's return to Jack and Martha for a minute. They had a great deal of debt, which prevented them from taking a vacation—at least, the kind of vacation Martha wanted— even though they both worked. The debt had accumulated over a number of years as the family lived beyond their income.

It turned out that the very same attitude that was driving Martha's anger about not being able to take a vacation had also helped to cause the debt. The attitude was *discontentment*. A woman's discontentment may come out in the form of comments like, "If we had an extra room where the kids could play, like Paul and Mary do, I could keep the family room clean." Discontentment can also be demonstrated through pervasive spending on the children or the house. Other signs may be a continual focus on what is still needed to make the family's life better or complete rather than gratitude for what the family already has. It may result in increasing Christmas spending each year, or buying things that aren't needed and are rarely used. Discontented wives might request things from their husbands, like Martha did, that they know they can't afford.

Wives, I'm not saying that you can't have desires or talk with your husband about your desires—after all, he might very well share those desires. But when you do, it should be clear to both that you're talking about *desires*—not *needs*. Too often, our desires are discussed so frequently that we begin to justify them as needs, even though the money isn't available to pay for them.

Ultimately, desires need to be set aside if they are clearly unattainable or foolish. However, if a desire becomes something you want in your life, you should begin to establish a plan to accomplish it. Chapter Fifteen talks about creating a vision for the family, establishing goals, and developing a plan to achieve your goals. Having common goals will create a strong marriage if you develop concrete plans (like a budget) to help you achieve your goals. All of this must be viewed from God's perspective. Not having a plan leaves the door open for each spouse to have different ideas for when and how these goals will be achieved, which frequently leads to disappointment, frustration, and anger.

Reading this book is probably a sign that you want to try another way. So, ladies, here are a few things you can do to fill your husband's significance tank:

- Let your husband know that you're willing to submit to a budget and that you'll support the process of developing one. *Do not nag him to start the process, but pray diligently for him and submit to his will.* While God is preparing your husband's heart to want to be on a budget and lead his family, examine your own heart and quietly become a better steward of what God has entrusted to you.

- If your husband agrees to live on a written budget, work with him to create a spending plan that you can both agree on. This will require submission, compromise, and change from you and a reliance on God's wisdom and strength—not your own.

- Willingly stay within your budget for those expense categories that you have control over.

- If it is necessary to keep your family spending below your income, willingly sacrifice your wants rather than telling your husband to sacrifice his (for example, give up having your nails done so that your husband can play golf once per month).

- Pray together before making financial decisions that would impact the budget and *do not move forward unless you are in agreement.*

- Meet with your husband at the end of *every* month to review and discuss the previous month's spending and income, regardless of who is paying the bills and doing the bookkeeping. Chapter Seventeen discusses this in more detail.

- Frequently thank your husband for being a hard worker and for providing for the family.

- Through all of this, allow your husband to lead. This can be petrifying when he continues to be selfish and is making unwise financial decisions. Remember that God loves you, that He is in control, and that He is your ultimate Provider.

- Learn, as all of us must, to be content (see Philippians 4:11–13). Complete the study on contentment at the end of this chapter with your husband.

Helping Your Wife to Feel Secure

The most common way that a man can make his wife feel insecure is by making financial decisions without her knowledge or consent.

Let me give you an example. Fred arrives home early one day from his job. Sara, a stay-at-home mom who home schools their two youngest children, asks Fred what's up. Fred shares that he finally decided that he'd had enough with his job and boss and decided to quit. Fred made this major financial decision without any input from his wife. He might have shared his dislike for his job, but this decision came as a total shock to Sara. Actually, it wasn't a total surprise to her, since Fred had made similar career choices without her concurrence before. Men, wives *do not* like spontaneity when it comes to big financial decisions. Especially when they intuitively know it is harmful to the family.

Not every man quits his job without first consulting his wife, but many men continually make spending decisions without the knowledge and consent of their wives. A husband who racks up charges on pay-per-view cable, buys a dog or big screen television, or joins a gym without his wife's knowledge and consent *slowly* undermines his wife's need for security. This is why it often takes fifteen to twenty years before a wife is ready to walk away from her marriage. A husbands can slowly dismantle his wife's confidence in him to keep her safe by unilaterally making financial decisions.

It's like the frog and boiling water story. If you put a frog in water at room temperature and slowly heat the water up, the frog will remain in the water unaware of the rising temperature because its body adjusts to the temperature change. By the time the water reaches a boil, the frog is dead. Too many husbands act like the Lone Ranger with regards to the family finances, ultimately resulting in wives who are emotionally dead.

The impact of a husband being the Lone Ranger is compounded when he turns the bookkeeping responsibilities over to his wife and shows no interest in knowing the details of their finances. They might say, "Honey, just pay the bills and everything will be fine." The insecurity issue doesn't necessarily become a problem if the family is saving money while all of this is going on. However, the *majority of families are not saving*. In fact, most of them are living beyond their income. This results in rising debt levels and late or missed payments on monthly bills. Guys, how do you think your wife feels when she doesn't have enough money to pay all the bills and you aren't involved enough to help find a godly solution? Does she feel secure or insecure?

In truth, your hands-off approach to finances makes her feel like an island, the storm waters pounding against her beachhead. She is dying inside. She may try to persevere for months, or even years, but the one thing that will surely bring out her anger is when her uninvolved husband gets angry with her for being late with a bill. At this point, the wife usually goes back to the desk, picks up the bills and checkbook, and calmly hands them over to her husband, saying, "You do it from now on!" Well, maybe she's not calm. This is also the point where she might begin to think that the marriage will never work.

The best thing for a husband to do at this point is to apologize for his unkind remarks. After all, as 1 Corinthians 13:4 says, *"Love is patient, love is kind and is not jealous; love does not brag and is not arrogant."* He should then make an appointment with the best Christian marriage counselor in the area—and with LifeChange Concepts!

Tom and Susan came to LifeChange Concepts for counseling after they were encouraged to do so by their marriage counselor. Susan was doing the bookkeeping, Mark was spending, debt was rising, and they had no savings. They were both in agreement that they needed to save for future needs and pay off debt, but Mark was clueless as to the impact his spending was having on the family finances, and he was beginning to play the blame game.

After they went through the process of discovering where their money went by completing a monthly income and expense form[4], they identified the attitudes that were behind their lifestyle decisions. At this point, Mark began to see the impact of his decision to give himself a $400 monthly allowance. Much to her credit, Susan said nothing, instead allowing the process of developing a spending plan under the guidance of a trained financial counselor to reveal the truth to her husband. It was so exciting to see them agree on a plan and then carry it out so that they could achieve the savings and debt elimination goals they both wanted.

So, guys, here are some things you can do in order to fill your wife's security tank:

- Let your wife know that you want to submit to a budget and then initiate the process of developing one with her.

- Work with your wife to create a spending plan that you can both agree on. This will require input from your wife (and maybe even older children) and compromise from both parties.

- Willingly stay within your budget for those expense categories that you have control over.

- If it is necessary to keep your family spending below your income, willingly sacrifice your wants rather than expecting your wife to do so (for example, give up golf so

---

[4] You can download the free form at my ministry website, www.lifechangeconcepts.org.

that your wife can get a babysitter for a couple of hours each week, giving her some much-needed alone time).

- Pray together before making financial decisions that would impact the budget and *do not move forward unless you are in agreement.*

- Meet with your wife at the end of *every* month to review and discuss the previous month's spending and income, regardless of who is paying the bills and doing the bookkeeping. Chapter Seventeen discusses this in more detail.

- Frequently tell your wife how much you value her input.

- Learn, as all of us must, to be content (see Philippians 4:11–13). See the study on contentment at the end of this chapter with your wife.

Key Point: Wives submitting to their husbands and husbands sacrificially loving their wives will be meeting their spouse's emotional needs and building oneness in their marriage.

Cultivating Oneness by Learning to Be Content

Do the following devotion on contentment together with your spouse:

1. In the following verses, what does God say we should be content with?

   - Luke 3:14
   - Philippians 4:11–12
   - 1 Timothy 6:8

2. In Philippians 4:11–12 the Apostle Paul said that he learned to be content in whatever circumstances he was in. Why did he (and you and I) have to learn to be content? (See Romans 3:23, Psalm 51:5, and Psalm 14:1–3)

3. What do the following verses tell you about God and why we should be content in all circumstances?

   - 1 Chronicles 29:11–12
   - Romans 8:28
   - Philippians 4:12–13
   - Philippians 4:19
   - Hebrews 13:5

4. What are the dangers of a covetous (i.e. greedy and materialistic) attitude?

   - 1 Timothy 6:9–10
   - Luke 12:13–21

5. How has the culture impacted the way you look at money and possessions?

6. How many of the following statements describe you?

    - You replace things that still have a useful life because you want the latest gadget or something better.

    - You spend your bonus (either literally or in your mind) months before you are due to get it.

    - You purchase another vehicle before or just after your current one is paid off.

    - You purchase items you either don't need or had no intention of buying when you went shopping.

    - You increase your Christmas spending each year.

    - Your credit card balances continue to rise even though you are making payments.

    - You have opened at least one new credit card account in the past twelve months without closing an existing account.

    - You have more than two credit cards.

    - You increase spending whenever your income increases.

    - You spend a lot of time thinking of ways to increase your income.

    - You spend more time thinking of what you need rather than enjoying what you have.

    - You verbally nag and complain about the things you don't have in your life.

    - You say yes quickly to new spending opportunities rather than praying for direction and seeking counsel from your spouse and others.

If you see yourself in some of these statements, you may have a contentment problem. Ask God and your spouse for forgiveness and ask for their help and encouragement as you learn to be content.

Additional Resources

Love & Respect, by Dr. Emerson Eggerichs

Ray Lynch

CHAPTER FOUR:
WHEN TRUST IS BROKEN

In this is love, not that we loved God, but that He loved us and sent His Son to be the propitiation for our sins.

1 John 4:10

Sin Revealed

It was around two o'clock in the morning when my wife awakened me from a deep sleep. Sobbing, she told me that she had been hiding something from me. Earlier that evening, we had attended the Wednesday evening service at our home church, Idlewild Baptist Church, and Pastor Whitten's message had convicted Judy that she needed to reveal to me a hidden part of her life.

During the next couple of hours, she explained to me that she had an eating addiction/disorder. She was eating fast food meals in addition to our three meals a day together. She was keeping her weight under control by purging. Even with the purging, her weight had increased noticeably since our wedding day nearly eleven years earlier. Her addiction had resulted in her lying to me and stealing from the family finances. She confessed her sins and asked for forgiveness, which was given. After receiving professional help at Remuda Ranch in Wickenburg, Arizona, Judy has been delivered from her addiction and our marriage is absolutely the best.

In counseling, I have observed dishonesty in marriage where the outcome was not resolved. For example, Samuel was a great salesman and, as with many great salesmen, he was poor with the details of money management. Over a period of eight years of exclusively handling the family finances, he allowed their credit card debt to reach $50,000. His wife, Rebecca, had never seen a credit card bill during this time. While he was away on a long business trip, Rebecca opened the monthly statements for two of the credit cards when they came in the mail. She was shocked to see two bills totaling more than $32,000—and even more shocked to learn that there was an additional $18,000 in debt. During their time with LifeChange Concepts, Samuel gave no indication of repentance, and Rebecca showed no forgiveness. This incident, combined with other unresolved trust issues, resulted in divorce a couple of years later.

Rebuilding Trust

All marriages are comprised of two imperfect people who will, to varying degrees, break the trust their spouse has put in them. Broken trust may be something big, like hiding accumulating credit card debt, or something smaller, like bouncing a check or making an unkind remark to your spouse in response to their input on a financial matter.

Because trust between a husband and wife is vital to having a strong and intimate marriage, it is important to repair broken trust. The problem then is not that we break trust, but that we don't repair it. The repair of broken trust is done through *repentance and confession* on the part of the spouse whose sin has resulted in broken trust and *forgiveness and reconciliation* on the part of the injured spouse. Together, they can begin the process of restoring trust.

However, if one or both are neglected, trust will remain damaged. As more and more trust-breaking situations go unresolved, the relationship will grow more distant. Conversely, if these situations are resolved in a biblical way, the marriage relationship usually grows more intimate. I am not so naïve as to believe that taking these two steps alone will resolve all situations where trust is broken. However, by implementing these disciplines into your marriage early and applying them to each trust-breaking incident, you will build a strong bridge of trust and intimacy that will be able to withstand a more challenging circumstance of broken trust.

Trust is broken every day, both in big ways and small ways. With each unkind remark I make to Judy, I undermine the trust she has in me to love her. Some of my unkind remarks may barely register on her "broken trust register," but they do register. It's like U.S. Senator Dierksen from Illinois said back in the 1960s when the U.S. Congress was looking for ways to balance the budget: "A million here and a million there, and before you know it you have real money." An unresolved broken trust here and an unresolved broken trust there, and before you know it you have a real problem in the marriage relationship.

Repentance and Confession

In his second letter to the saints of Corinth, Paul wrote to them that he was pleased with the way they had responded to his earlier rebuke of their sinful actions, given in his first letter. Paul said,

> *I now rejoice, not that you were made sorrowful, but that you were made sorrowful to the point of repentance; for you were made sorrowful according to the will of God, so that you might not suffer loss in anything through us. For the sorrow that is according to the will of God produces a repentance without regret, leading to salvation, but the sorrow of the world produces death.*
>
> *2 Corinthians 7:9–10*

The saints at the church of Corinth were convicted (i.e. with godly sorrow) by Paul's rebuke, which then produced repentance and confession. Conviction of our sins, leading to repentance, is often the result of God's Word speaking to our hearts. Psalm 38:4 says, *"My guilt has overwhelmed me like a burden too heavy to bear"* (NIV). Unconfessed sin is like a heavy weight on our shoulders. God desires this heavy weight, or conviction, to lead to repentance and confession. Psalm 38:18 says, *"I confess my iniquity; I am troubled by my sin"* (NIV).

Jay E. Adams, in his book *How to Help People Change*, defines confession as "a sinner's acknowledgment of his guilt against another in order to seek his forgiveness and achieve reconciliation."[5] When I confess to Judy godly sorrow for an unkind remark, I demonstrate a pattern of repentance and confession that acknowledges that I care about her and our relationship and that I will not desert her.

In contrast to the godly sorrow produced in the Corinthians, the writer of Hebrews gives the example of Esau: "When he desired to inherit the blessing, he was rejected, for he found no place for repentance, though he sought for it with tears" (Hebrews 12:17).

---

[5] Adams, Jay E. *How to Help People Change* (Grand Rapids, MI: Zondervan, 1986), p. 150.

Esau's worldly sorrow resulted in tears, but no repentance. It was more a show for sympathy than a confession of sin.

During the 1970s, someone came out with a cute little book that defined love through a series of single sentence descriptions. One of these stated that love "is never having to say you are sorry." On the surface, this may appear to some as a valid description of what love is. Their logic goes something like this: if your love is true, then you don't have to say you are sorry when you hurt your spouse, because they know your love is true. In truth, this is not biblical love. True biblical love will always result in an apology when one spouse has hurt the other. Whereas Judy was convicted of her sin and repented to both God and me, Samuel never gave any indication of repentance and his apology was more like many public figures who have expressed regret over their actions once those actions became public knowledge. This is a "sorry I got caught" apology, which rings hollow and empty, rather than a "sorry I sinned and hurt you" apology. All of us have received these types of apologies in our lifetimes and we can usually see the lack of sincerity in them.

Confession is not general, but specific. As you read through this book and the scriptures reveal your sins, you'll find that it's time to repent and confess specifically, not only to your spouse but to God. As King David correctly noted in his repentant Psalm 51 (for his sin with Bathsheba), "Against You, You only, I have sinned and done what is evil in Your sight" (Psalm 51:4). Upon his return home, the Prodigal Son said to his father, "I have sinned against heaven, and in your sight" (Luke 15:18). The wonderful thing about confessing our sins to God is that He always forgives us, even if our spouse does not. 1 John 1:9 says, "If we confess our sins, He is faithful and righteous to forgive us our sins and to cleanse us from all unrighteousness." Isaiah 55:7 says, "Let the wicked forsake his way and the evil man his thoughts. Let him turn to the Lord, and he will have mercy on him, and to our God, for he will freely pardon" (NIV). Just as the Prodigal Son's father was quick to forgive and restore him, so is God.

An all too frequent happening in the counseling room is one spouse saying very unkind things to the other. This often results in reciprocation. The war of words usually continues for a minute or two ending, when each person is satisfied that they have won the battle. I often wonder how bad it gets in private if they are comfortable with saying these hurtful things in my presence. After one particularly bad session with a couple, where three of these battles took place, I considered the total lack of remorse shown by either person. Their unkind and hurtful words were sins against God and their mate, yet there was no indication that they were even aware of this.

In my twenty-two years of counseling I have only had a few husbands or wives apologize for their unkind words in my presence. Granted, they may do it later. For most, however, the apology never takes place. Our unconfessed sins continue to pile up in our marriages, where they quietly work behind the scenes to bring the marriage down.

> *He who conceals his sins does not prosper, but whoever confesses and renounces them finds mercy.*
> *Proverbs 28:13, NIV*

Forgiveness and Reconciliation

Once you have confessed you sin to your spouse, you must then ask your spouse for his or her forgiveness. Forgiveness and reconciliation are important to both parties because it brings about closure and allows for healing. However, even if your spouse refuses to forgive you, you can have closure because of God's forgiveness.

In his letter to the church at Colosse, the Apostle Paul wrote about putting on the new self (see Colossians 3:1–17). In these verses, he outlines a contrast between the members of one's earthly body, where a person walks before our salvation, and one's *new self who is being renewed to a true knowledge according to the image of the One who created him"* (Colossians 3:10). The former self walked in disobedience: immorality, impurity, passion, evil desire, greed, anger, wrath, malice, slander, and abusive speech. In contrast, he said that *"since you **laid aside** the old self with its evil practices, and **have put on the new self"*** (Colossians 9–10, emphasis added) you have *"put on a heart of compassion, kindness, humility, gentleness and patience; bearing with one another, and **forgiving each other**... Just as the Lord forgave you, so also should you"* (Colossians 3:12–13). Paul says that because we have been raised up with Christ, we have put on the new self, which empowers us to forgive others.

When our focus is on heavenly things and we are yielding to the Holy Spirit, we will bear *"the fruit of the Spirit [which] is love, joy, peace, patience, kindness, goodness, faithfulness, gentleness, self-control..."* (Galatians 5:22–23). As a result, our relationships will thrive.

Why do we forgive? We forgive each other because God has forgiven us. I was not born again until I was thirty-nine years old, and because of the damage I did to others in my life, I have a pretty good understanding of what grace and forgiveness are. God unconditionally forgave *all* my sins so that I can abide in heaven with Him forever. If you are born of the Spirit, do you understand how valuable this gift of salvation is? Need I remind you that we all deserve hell, eternal separation from God? Paul referred to this gift as *"the riches of His grace which He lavished on us"* (Ephesians 1:7–8).

Not forgiving your spouse who has hurt you is disobedience on your part, and you will one day be accountable before a holy, all-knowing God for this sin. It will not keep you out of heaven, but it will reduce the crowns you have to place at Jesus' feet. In addition, it will make life less abundant for you on earth.

Some people believe that by not forgiving their spouse, they can exercise control over them… and isn't control what we want when we have been hurt? By not forgiving them, we can make them feel guilty. The only problem is they don't feel guilty. Your unwillingness to forgive and the games you play, such as frequently bringing up their misdeeds or giving them the silent treatment, will make them feel angry, not guilty, and further jeopardize oneness in your marriage.

What Would You Do?

If you discovered that your wife had a large amount of credit card debt that she had hidden from you, what would you do? What if your husband had not paid the mortgage for three months when you thought he had, or if your wife bought something of significant value that you couldn't afford without your knowledge? Would you forgive your spouse? What if they didn't apologize; would you forgive them? Would there be a difference in the way you responded if your spouse revealed the situation and confessed their wrong before you discovered it? What if they had done this twice, or three times? Would you base your willful choice to forgive on the size of the crime, the degree of your spouse's repentance, or the number of times it happened rather than the command from the Bible?

> *But God demonstrates His own love toward us, in that while we were yet sinners, Christ died for us.*
>
> *Romans 5:8*

The Big Hurt

Too often, a husband or wife will hurt their spouse (a bad thing) and then apologize (a good thing) without understanding the depth of the hurt they have done to their spouse (a bad thing). When this happens, the spouse who has been hurt may accept the apology and forgive their mate, but they do so with a strong sense that the apology was hollow and that the same hurt will occur again.

I believe that this is how Shirley, who I mentioned earlier, felt about Bob's apologies. The truth is that those who feel this way are correct. Why? David Ferguson, a Christian therapist, author, and speaker, believes that until the person who administered the hurt understands the depth of the hurt, they will probably not be changed and therefore are likely to hurt their spouse in the same way again. Conversely, if they understand with empathy the damage of their sin against their spouse, they are less likely to hurt their spouse again, and the injured spouse will know this.

This means that if you have seriously broken the trust of your spouse, like Bob did to Shirley (David Ferguson calls this "the big hurt"), you will need to sit down with your spouse and ask them to share how they were hurt. You can say nothing the entire time, except to ask for clarification or to confirm that you understand. You can leave your defense attorney at home. You cannot question your spouse's feeling, because whatever they are feeling is valid. Your role is to listen and understand how deeply you have hurt the one you love. This sharing may take twenty minutes or two hours.

During a class for engaged couples I co-taught at Idlewild Baptist Church, we used a video series by David Ferguson. His message about "the big hurt" hit me squarely between the eyes. I realized that I had hurt Judy deeply on our wedding day and had never allowed her to express her hurt. The big hurt was that I had made the decision to take my children (ages eight and six at the time) along on our one-day honeymoon to the beach. Because of their ages, we all slept in the same room together. I have done many dumb things in my life, but this one tops them all. Fourteen years of marriage transpired since that day of bad judgment without even an apology.

On the way home from church after this class, I used what I had learned from David Ferguson. I told Judy that I realized for the first time how deeply I had probably hurt her that day and that I wanted her to communicate to me how she had felt because of my decision. As she did, I wept inside as I understood how badly I had hurt the one I love. After she finished, I apologized and asked her for her forgiveness. My apology was authentic because I understood the pain I had inflicted on her. Her forgiveness was authentic because she saw my repentant heart.

Boundaries After Forgiveness

In the area of finances, forgiveness does not necessarily mean that everything will return to the way it was before the sin. In many cases, financial accountability may have to accompany marriage counseling to help rebuild trust. Forgiveness is *not* about condoning what your spouse did or allowing the injustice to continue.

Jim and Ann came to me because Jim had had an adulterous affair during which he had accumulated over $30,000 in credit card debt. Ann had forgiven Jim, but she required that they see marriage and financial counselors and that he close the credit card account. My role was not only to help them establish a budget and share the truths of God's Word on money; more importantly, I was there to be their accountability partner as Ann rebuilt her trust in Jim. We met for two years, and in that time Jim faithfully paid down much of the credit card debt and learned to better communicate money matters with Ann.

It is not a question of *if* we will do something financially hurtful to our spouse, but *when.* If you choose to withhold forgiveness from your spouse, you allow sin to build up in you. Hebrews 12:1 says, *"Therefore, since we have so great a cloud of witnesses surrounding us, let us also lay aside every encumbrance and the sin which so easily entangles us."* It is difficult to run the race of life when we are weighed down by the sin of unforgiveness.

Lessons for the Injured Spouse

I learned a valuable lesson during the incident with my wife's eating addiction. God also wants to teach the injured spouse something. Why? Because injured spouses are imperfect people who God is trying to conform to His image. Out of Judy's struggle, God taught me two things about myself that needed to be changed.

At the time of the incident, we didn't have health insurance, so we applied for a scholarship from Remuda Ranch. A few days after our request, we received a call indicating that we had been denied and that we would have to pay the $72,000 bill ourselves. The reason they reached this decision was because of an IRA I'd had from before our marriage which held enough funds to pay the bill. I didn't hesitate to tell them that we would pay the bill, because I love my wife and she needed their help. Her health and our marriage were more important than that money.

A few days after our decision to move forward with the treatment, during my morning quiet time with the Lord, He revealed my first sin to me. God exposed the idolatry and pride in my heart, as I had been spending far too much time viewing my growing IRA balance. My trust in it had reached a point of serious concern to Him. With a broken spirit, I confessed my sin to the

Lord and later to my wife at breakfast. How wonderful it felt as each of them forgave me.

The second sin God revealed to me came directly from Judy. During her healing time at Remuda Ranch, she shared with me her feelings about me often trying to fix her. She felt that I wanted her to be someone that she wasn't and never would be. Did I love her? Did I believe that God had brought us together? If so, why was I trying to change her? These questions and others raced through my mind as Judy openly and honestly shared her heart with me. This was a major turning point in our marriage, as God revealed this sin to me and I confessed my sin, apologized, and asked for forgiveness. I am much improved in this area, but I am thankful for a wife who did not expect me to change overnight and has continued to accept my apologies.

When we forgive our spouse, our hearts are free to be open to hear what God wants to reveal to us. Then, as we receive His gentle correction, we can grow more like Him. The final result is a marriage where each partner is growing more Christ-like and the marriage is getting better and better.

As I said before, our marriage is so much better because of that crisis. We both thank God for it.

> **Key Point: A marriage cannot reach greatness without ongoing repentance/confession and forgiveness/ reconciliation.**

Cultivating Oneness through Confession and Forgiveness

1. When was the last time you apologized to your spouse for a rude comment you made towards them? Do you just brush it off with a thought like, "That's the way she talks to me," "It wasn't that big a deal," "She has probably forgotten about it anyway," or some other justification for not getting right with her and God? If you have stopped apologizing for the small unkind things you say to your spouse, you will be less likely to apologize for a larger infraction. Think back to your last offense against your spouse. If you did not apologize and ask for forgiveness, you need to do so.

2. Has your spouse apologized for something they did and you have not forgiven them? Forgiveness is not a weakness, but a sign of strength and maturity. Cast off the bitterness and anger you have been holding onto, go to your spouse, and express your forgiveness. In doing so, identify the offense that you are forgiving.

3. If your spouse is behaving in an unbiblical way towards you (like me trying to fix Judy), speak with your spouse about it. Before having the conversation, pray for God's direction and the words to say, as well as for your spouse's heart to be prepared for what you will say. Speak about how his or her actions make you feel, rather than trying to place blame. Finally, read the book of Esther to see how she handled a similar situation.

Additional Resources
How to Help People Change, by Jay E. Adams.

CHAPTER FIVE:
ONENESS ENHANCERS

My beloved is mine, and I am his.

Song of Solomon 2:16

In this chapter, I want to look at what I call oneness enhancers: prayer, good communication, dreaming, and laughter. These are skills and disciplines that, when incorporated into your finances, will enhance your whole marriage relationship.

Prayer

Numerous studies have found that the happiest couples are those who pray together. Not only are these couples happier, but they are also more likely to describe their marriages as being highly romantic.

In my twenty-two years of counseling, I have seen my share of unhappy couples. I once received an email from a wife who took my Growing Financial Stewards God's Way class with her husband which best describes how many couples feel towards each other. She said,

Before we started your class, we were in a really bad place financially, spiritually, and emotionally. Our marriage was not happy and we were not only frustrated with one another, but openly unkind to one another. We are grateful that the class was not only about finances, but also about the dynamics of finances in a marriage.

This couple, as well as with most unhappy couples I have counseled, prayed together very infrequently. Prayer, and particularly vulnerable prayer, is the most important discipline for creating oneness in marriage, whether with finances or any other marital aspect. Again, I must confess that praying together was a very random activity for Judy and me during the first twelve years of our marriage. We were very active Christians during this period, attending Bible studies, teaching, doing bus ministry, visiting those in need, singing in the choir (Judy, not me), ushering, and on and on. However, I have learned that no amount of being "religious" can make up for the time we spend in shared prayer.

While teaching the Engaged Couples class at Idlewild Baptist Church, the Lord convicted me of this deficiency in our marriage. After repenting to the Lord and to Judy, we decided to begin praying together once per week. We selected a night that rarely had activity and began a discipline that we have faithfully maintained these past nine years. It's not a coincidence that our relationship has grown more intimate, our oneness in finances is greater, and other areas of our marriage have grown stronger during this period. We have established our prayer night as sacred time and make sure we schedule around it.

In addition to this weekly prayer time, I also began praying over Judy every morning before either of us started our workday. Actually, we lock ourselves together in a great big bear hug and I pray for her and thank God for her. We had been doing this for a number of years when I began to think that she enjoyed the hug time more than the prayers. Boy was I wrong! One morning, I got out of the house without our prayer time and that night she informed me that she had really missed my prayers for her and had felt out of sorts for the entire day. I vowed to never miss a day again.

Shared prayer that focuses on the almightiness of God, that gives thanks for everything, and is humble and gentle (see Ephesians 4:2) will bring you to shared holy ground. It will create a oneness that will carry your relationship to levels of intimacy and trust you think are only found in fairy tales. Therefore, I encourage you to find time to have prayer with your spouse at least once per week.

Good Communication

The Bible tells us, *"By wisdom a house is built, and by understanding it is established"* (Proverbs 24:3). Proper communication is necessary in order to have understanding. Just uttering words does not mean communication is taking place. In order to have solid communication with understanding, three components must be present: expressing, listening, and responding.

In their book *Saving Your Marriage Before It Starts*, Dr. Les Parrott III and Dr. Leslie Parrott share that "97 percent of those who rated their communication with their spouse as excellent were happily married, compared to only 56 percent who rated their communication as poor."[6] A couple's ability to communicate well is vital to a stable and satisfying marriage.

Expressing. The purpose of this book is not to teach you how to be an effective communicator or how to handle conflict. There are plenty of excellent books already in print for that. As previously

---

[6] Parrott III, Les and Leslie Parrott. *Saving Your Marriage Before It Begins* (Grand Rapids, MI: Zondervan, 1995), p. 73.

mentioned, the Parrotts' book can give you skills to help you express your feelings, ideas, and plans in ways that will strengthen your marriage. In light of that, I only want to look at a couple of inappropriate ways to communicate that I have observed in the counseling room: control tactics and unilateral decision making.

1. **Control Tactics:** When you're discussing a financial issue, avoid using controlling tactics. Unfortunately, most couples know what to say or do in order to get their spouse to agree with them. We use guilt, blame, silence, pouting, and yelling. Wives use the "significance button" on their husbands (see Chapter Three) and husbands play the "I'm the spiritual leader" card in ways beyond God's intent... all in order to move our mate towards our desired solution. At times, we will even get "historical," by bringing up the past, to win our case. Initially, you need to stick to the facts of the issue at hand so that the Holy Spirit and the study of God's Word can have time to work on both of your hearts.

   To help you evaluate your communicative approach, I have provided a financial scenario below for you and your spouse to work through:

Scenario One

You receive a phone call from your married brother. He informs you that his electric and cell phone bills are two months behind and service will be shut off unless they are paid within two days. He needs $340 to get caught up. He also informs you that he is only calling you for help because their five credit cards are maxed out and they have nowhere else to turn. He also tells you that they are behind because his overtime at work was cut two months ago.

As he makes his request, you remember that you paid their car payment eight months earlier when again his overtime was cut. He reminds you how cold it will get in their apartment if the electricity is shut off, and that this would not be good for their two-year-old daughter. Money is not an issue for you, since your family finances are in great shape and you have a great deal of savings. Stop reading now and role-play this financial scenario with your spouse.

How did you handle this situation? Did you discuss the issue with your spouse? Did you make a decision without consulting your spouse? Did you explain the situation to your spouse and then tell them what you were going to do without their input? Did you remind your spouse that you had just helped his or her parents three months ago? Did you communicate the facts and suggest that you both take some time to pray about what God wants you to do with His money?

2. **Unilateral Decisions:** Another problem I often see with couples regarding communication is the lack of it. I'm not talking about occasional forgetfulness, which we all have. I'm talking about the willful decision to not tell your spouse about a purchase you want to make or have already made (hiding). Most times, this selective forgetfulness or failure to communicate is done because you know your spouse will disagree with your plan or purchase. Avoiding the conflict (fear) and just doing what you want (selfishness) seems to be a better idea to many in this situation. In truth, this approach generally increases distrust in your marriage and takes you further away from oneness.

Using what you learned in Chapters Three and Four can help build trust and cultivate oneness with your finances. Below is a financial scenario involving a unilateral decision made by the husband (the roles could very easily be reversed). Role-play this scenario with your spouse to see how you would handle the situation.

> ### Scenario Two
>
> While at Best Buy, your husband noticed an incredible sale on a flat-screen TV that had been returned by another customer. He decided to purchase it, knowing that it would be a nice surprise for you. The two of you had talked about getting one but had agreed to wait another year, because you were saving money for airline tickets to see your family at Christmas. Your husband felt the bargain was too good to pass up and that he had to make the decision himself, since you were in a conference and could not be reached and the TV would probably be sold very soon.

Listening. If you want to learn how *not* to communicate, just watch a TV talk show when it has two people of opposing views debating a subject. Rudeness prevails, with each person interrupting and trying to shout over the other person. I can usually watch about ten seconds of this and then I flip to another channel. It's even crazier when there are three or four people involved in the discussion.

I am a self-confessed better talker than listener, and the Lord continues to refine me in this area. James 1:19 says, *"This you know, my beloved brethren. But everyone must be quick to hear, slow to speak and slow to anger."* Notice that the verse says to be quick to *hear.* Not talking while another person is talking does not necessarily mean that you are hearing what that person is saying. In truth, many times we use the time when another person is talking to put together in our minds what we are going to say next. James tells us that we need to hear (understand) what our spouse is saying. To better understand what our spouse is expressing to us, we must become active listeners.

The following skills will help you to be an active listener.

- Restating: This is a process in which you repeat what your spouse has said but with emphasis on specifics of content and feelings. For example, how could you restate the following statement from your spouse? Spouse, in a slightly frustrated tone of voice: "We need to save money for our daughter's college, but I really want to go on a family vacation. I want to do both but can't see how we can achieve it. What should we do?" Restating content and feelings may go like this: "You would like to save for our daughter's college and go on a family vacation... and you are frustrated about it."

- Paraphrasing: This is a process of taking the essential content of your spouse's communication and restating it in your own words. Again, like restating, there can be an emphasis on content and feelings.

- Minimal Encouragers: Minimal encouragers, or conversational responses, are used to keep your spouse talking (though some of us don't need this in order to keep us talking). More importantly, minimal encouragers let them know that you are listening. We use them all the time without realizing it, and therefore they're one of the easier active listening techniques to master. Examples of verbal minimal encouragers are: "I see," "Okay," and "Uh-huh" (though I think my eighth-grade English teacher would dislike this last example). An example of nonverbal encouragement would be nodding your head.

- Open-Ended Questions: These questions require your spouse to give an answer other than yes or no. They encourage your spouse to talk and express their thoughts, feelings, and ideas. "Why" questions should be avoided, however, because they tend to put people on the defensive. Questions that start with "what," "how," and "when" are all good.

Finally, since our body language, facial expressions, and tone, rate, and volume of our verbal communication often conveys our true message, it's important to take these factors into consideration as you listen to your mate.

Responding. At some point in almost every conversation, you need to move beyond listening. You need to join the conversation and seek to truly understand what your spouse is saying. Dr. James Dobson of Focus on the Family illustrated this by saying that conversation is like two people playing tennis. One player hits the ball over the net and the other player hits it back. The conversation would end very quickly if only one person talked and the other only listened.

Remember what it says in James 1:19—be slow to speak. When we do respond, it needs to be the appropriate response at the appropriate time. One technique I have begun to use in order to speak at the appropriate time is to wait for a lull in the action before speaking. I will wait four to five seconds, which can seem like an eternity, before responding. This helps protect me from interrupting Judy in the event that she is just pausing to gather her thoughts before saying something more.

Staying on topic and trying to better understand your spouse's expression by using active listening techniques would be an appropriate response to encourage communication. Shifting a conversation about finances to NFL football would not be an appropriate response. Another bad response to your spouse's expressions about problems in their life may be to offer solutions. For example, Judy sometimes comes home from work and expresses difficult things that happen to her that day. Early in our marriage, I would immediately offer solutions, not realizing that most of the time she just wanted me to listen. Now, if I'm not sure whether she wants me to "just listen" or offer solutions, I'll ask her what she wants me to do. Since this is the goal of communication—to understand your mate—this is an appropriate response.

The three components to basic communication—expressing, listening, and responding—may sound simple, but mastering them is a lifelong challenge! Like any new skill, they require lots of practice. But the important thing is that you get started and keep at it.

Practice Exercise

A question I have often asked couples during counseling is, "What things about your spouse make you feel insecure about your financial future?" Using the skills above ask this question to your spouse and see how much you can learn about yourself.

Dreaming

In Chapter Fifteen, I will discuss setting financial goals for the family. Financial goals are good and will help to cultivate oneness in your finances. However, dreaming together is just as important towards cultivating oneness. A dream doesn't even start out as a goal, but if it is the Lord's will, it will move into the goal category at some point, and then the planning will begin.

Judy and I dream of going to Ireland for vacation or renting an RV for a couple of months and traveling around America. Some dreams fall to the wayside for practical reasons, like lack of money or poor health. For example, my dream of participating in a sprint triathlon was dashed by a hip made sore by running. Many dreams will just make good conversation and go nowhere.

It's okay to talk about our dreams from time to time, but they should not become a frequent topic of discussion unless they have moved into the goal category. Taking too much time to dwell on your dreams can lead to a covetous heart, and as I will share in Chapter Seven, that's not good for your finances or your marriage. Having dreams and aspirations is healthy, because it gives us something to hope for. Just as dreaming of being in heaven with Jesus someday helps us through the difficult times of our lives, so our other dreams help to strengthen our relationship.

A note of caution: when you first start expressing your dreams to your spouse, make sure that they understand that you are just dreaming. The last thing you need is for them to go out and rent an RV for a couple of months if that is not really feasible for your budget.

Laughter

When was the last time you and your spouse laughed about something? I mean laughed so hard your sides hurt. Are you able to laugh about past financial decisions that turned out poorly, or do you instead harbor grudges or anger towards your spouse for putting you in those situations? I'm not talking about decisions that significantly hurt the family financially. Do things like a vacation gone badly or running out of gas while on a trip because one spouse decided to wait until the next exit to fill up bring on laughter or anger?

For a few years, my wife and I didn't have money for an annual vacation, so we would go to timeshare presentations in Williamsburg, Virginia, which was our favorite place to visit. The timeshare company would pay for a room for two nights and give us fifty dollars in exchange for listening to a one-hour presentation. We would pack a cooler of food and head to Williamsburg with no intent of buying a timeshare.

The third time we did this, I went brain-dead during the sales pitch. It was either that, or the salesperson was quite good. Whatever the case, when it came time for the close, I was ready to sign on the dotted line.

If looks could kill, I would have been dead. Obviously, my wife was thinking throughout the sales pitch about getting out of there and going over to the restored Colonial Williamsburg area just as we had done the two previous times. She was in shock. She thought my babblings during the session of how we could make money on this deal was my way of having fun with the salesperson.

Unfortunately, I had our checkbook with me. Before you could say lickety split, the contract was signed. I must confess that the next eighteen hours weren't fun. God hammered me unmercifully and Judy kept muttering that she couldn't believe I had done it. After hours of beating myself up for making a foolish decision and a sleepless night, we returned to the scene of the crime and requested that the contract be voided (by law, we had three days to do this). The only thing worse than sitting through a one-hour time share sales pitch is sitting through a two-hour, pressure-packed sales pitch to encourage you to keep the timeshare!

Judy and I have laughed about this incident so many times over the past fourteen years since it happened. I don't think we would be laughing if we hadn't been able to get out of the contract. She has never used this lack of good judgment as a club against me, but instead continues to share the humor of this story with me.

Earlier in our marriage, when funds were limited, I was also known for putting us up in some rather unsavory motels during our trips to

Florida to visit my father. We once stayed in a motel in Starke, Florida where we felt it necessary to back our van up against the motel door to make it difficult for someone to break into it. To make matters worse, we were kept up all night listening to passing trains on the railroad tracks that were about fifteen yards from our broken bathroom window. Retelling this story still brings tears of laughter.

If your marriage is being strained by finances and you aren't happy about it, it's time to laugh. Grab a cup of coffee or iced tea, sit down with your spouse, and begin to replay those laughable times in your life. Alternate sharing stories without malice or blame and begin to laugh. If you've never laughed or haven't laughed in a long time, it may take a while to prime the pump. Was it a camping trip gone bad or the oversized station wagon you almost bought? Relax, take your time, and the stories will come to you. Then laugh, laugh at yourself, and laugh hard.

> *A joyful heart is good medicine, but a broken spirit dries up the bones.*
>
> *Proverbs 17:22*

Key Point: There is no other discipline that will strengthen a marriage greater than a couple transparently and humbly praying together on a regular, ongoing basis.

Cultivating Oneness through Prayer, Good Communication, Dreaming, and Laughter

1. Discuss with your spouse about having a weekly prayer time together, then set a time that is convenient for both of you. Keep this time sacred by blocking it out on the calendar and scheduling around it. If something else preempts this time, set another time for that week's prayer. Be sure to write out your prayer requests so that you can continue to pray for them each week until God answers.

2. How did you do working through Scenarios One and Two? Were you able to find common ground and strengthen your relationship in the process? Did you discover your personal strengths and challenges when it comes to effective communication?

3. Each of you write down two dreams you have (e.g. where you would like to go on your thirtieth wedding anniversary) and then discuss with your spouse why this is one of your dreams.

4. Recount a story of something funny that happened in your marriage. Have the one to whom the laughter is targeted tell the story. Poking fun at yourself can be therapeutic.

Additional Resources

Saving Your Marriage Before It Starts, by Les Parrott III and Leslie Parrott.

Many things are involved in cultivating financial oneness. As a married couple, we become "one" under Christ's headship, and that includes all aspects of our married life. The financial aspect is one of the most critical for many couples, so it is important to be purposeful and deliberate in creating a spirit of oneness in this area.

We never make substantial purchases without first consulting with each other and coming to a decision as to whether we should make that purchase and what the cost should be. Although we may put those purchases on our one and only credit card (to get the benefit of flight miles), we always pay off our credit card in full each month, leaving no balance and eliminating debt. "Submit to one another out of reverence for Christ" *(Ephesians 5:21, NIV).*

As in all things, prayer is the best resource for oneness in all parts of our lives, including finances. So, prayer for God's direction in our lives is very important. "And my God will meet all your needs according to his glorious riches in Christ Jesus" *(Philippians 4:19).*

—John and Terry Harris
Bethesda, MD

Ray Lynch

CHAPTER SIX:
THE FOUNDATION

Therefore everyone who hears these words of Mine and acts on them, may be compared to a wise man who built his house on the rock.

Matthew 7:24

The Bible says, "All Scripture is inspired by God and profitable for teaching, for reproof, for correction, for training in righteousness; so that the man of God may be adequate, equipped for every good work" (2 Timothy 3:16–17). God has provided to humankind the operating manual for life. This manual, the Holy Bible, tells of God and His attributes of holiness, sovereignty, and love. It also tells about our human nature of sin, explaining how we can obtain eternal life with God. In addition, the Bible teaches us how we can achieve spiritual maturity after we are saved. The scriptures equip us to live a righteous, spirit-filled life resulting in love, joy, and peace (see Galatians 5:22).

God's Book on Finances

This same book also shows us how to manage our finances. In fact, the Bible says more about financial matters and possessions than any other subject except love. Sixteen of the thirty-eight parables teach a lesson regarding how to handle money and possessions. In the four gospels, one out of every ten verses deals with the subject of money.

So, why did God devote so much of the Bible to financial matters? I believe He did so for two reasons.

First, He did it for *His preeminence*. The very first of the Ten Commandments was, *"You shall have no other gods before Me"* (Exodus 20:3). Things like houses, cars, investments, jobs, credit cards, and children can become gods that distract us from the worship of and service to God. Jesus made this point when He said, *"No one can serve two masters; for either he will hate the one and love the other, or he will be devoted to the one and despise the other. You cannot serve God and wealth"* (Matthew 6:24). It is humanly impossible to love and serve God and money at the same time. James was even more direct when he wrote, *"Therefore whoever wishes to be a friend of the world makes himself an enemy of God"* (James 4:4).

There is a way in which we can manage the money and possessions God has entrusted to us that will demonstrate God's preeminence in our lives. The Bible tells us all about it, and this book will highlight these important truths.

The second reason that God devoted so much of the Bible to financial matters is for *our protection*. God loves us deeply and has no desire to see us fail. Therefore, He has given us commands and principles, which I will call *God's Way*, to help us navigate through life victoriously. In Matthew 7:24–27, Jesus concludes His Sermon on the Mount by telling the story of two homebuilders. One built his home on the sand (World's Way) while the other built his on the rock (God's Way). Jesus labeled the former a fool and the latter a wise man. Jesus used this illustration to say, "Look, I just poured out my heart to you. I gave you incredible truths about life. If you don't apply them to your life, you are a fool." God's commands and principles on money management always work.

This doesn't mean that we won't go through difficult times, because God says we will, but it does mean that following God's Word on money will give us peace and strength when going through those difficult times.

Commands and Principles

Of the over two thousand verses in the Bible dealing with finances, there is only one command given: pay your taxes. However, there are many principles. Let me give an example of a principle. Proverbs 21:20 says, *"There is desirable treasure, and oil in the dwelling of the wise, but a foolish man squanders it"* (NKJV) This principle says that the wise man saves, but the foolish man doesn't. If this had been a command, it may have said, "Thou shall save ten percent of your income." Whereas a command is very clear, the principle leaves unanswered questions—such as, how much do I need to save in order to be wise?

Why didn't God just give us the Ten Commandments for money? Because by giving us principles instead of commands, God:

- acknowledges that the world of finances is not all black and white;

- reminds us that He created us uniquely (see Chapter 2); and

- knows that by not giving us clear direction (i.e. commandments) in our finances, we will have to come to Him in prayer to seek clarity.

Prayer is a vital component of being a good and faithful steward of God's resources and cultivating oneness in your marriage. Remember, God wants to be preeminent in our lives, and we can remind ourselves of this by consulting with Him daily regarding financial issues.

Foundational Truths

There are a few foundational truths which establish the context by which everything that is said in the Bible about money and possessions should be interpreted.

The first is that God is the Owner of everything we have, and as a result we are just managers of His property. Psalm 24:1 says, "The earth is the Lord's, and all it contains, the world, and those who dwell in it." When we believe in our hearts that we really don't own anything, that everything we have is God's, we will handle all that has been entrusted to us by God differently. Randy Alcorn, founder and director of Eternal Perspective Ministries, believes that all financial decisions become spiritual decisions once you come to believe in your heart that everything is owned by God.

The Apostle Paul wrote, "Whether, then, you eat or drink or whatever you do, do all to the glory of God" (1 Corinthians 10:31). Does the way you handle the resources God has entrusted to you glorify Him? Does the way you handle the resources God has entrusted to you bring you and your family, friends, and coworkers closer to God or take you further away? Understanding that every financial decision has eternal ramifications should cause concern for those who are going through life on autopilot, rarely consulting with God, their spouse, or other godly counsel.

The second truth is that God is sovereign and in control, not us. According to 1 Chronicles 29:11–12,

Everything in the heavens and earth is Yours, oh Lord, and this is Your kingdom. We adore You as being in control of everything. Riches and honor come from You alone, and You are the Ruler of all mankind. Your hand controls power and might, and it is at Your discretion that men are made great and are given strength. (TLB)

Do you believe this? Do you adore God as being in control of everything? When "life" happens, do you get frustrated and angry, or do you praise God as Job did after he had lost everything? Do you believe that how much you make is in God's control, not yours? How many husbands and wives are working ungodly hours month after month and are having little or no influence on the upbringing of their children? Do you believe that God is sovereign and in control when you lose your job or have to take a pay cut? God has given us personal responsibility for our choices, but His sovereignty gives Him the right to make some people great and others not, regardless of our choices.

We have no say in what circumstances we will encounter in our lifetimes, but we do have a say in how we respond to those circumstances. Habakkuk, the minor prophet, describes an economy in Judah that was very similar to the American economy in recent years:

Though the fig tree should not blossom and there be no fruit on the vines, though the yield of the olive should fail and the fields produce no food, though the flock should be cut off from the fold and there be no cattle in the stalls…

Habakkuk 3:17

So, how did the prophet respond to his difficult situation? Let's continue reading:

> *...yet I will exult in the Lord, I will rejoice in the God of my salvation. The Lord God is my strength, and He has made my feet like hinds' feet, and makes me walk on my high places.*
> *Habakkuk 3:18–19*

God made hinds, a deer-like animal, to be able to easily navigate rocky, mountainous terrain so that they could outmaneuver their predators. In the same way, God is our strength, our protector, our Savior, and we can rejoice in the Lord even when life throws us a curve.

In the end, our Sovereign God cares more about our obedience to Him than He does our busyness for Him. The prophet Samuel told a disobedient King Saul, *"Has the Lord as much delight in burnt offerings and sacrifices as in obeying the voice of the Lord? Behold, to obey is better than sacrifice, and to heed than the fat of rams"* (1 Samuel 15:22). Are you obediently managing the money God has given to you or, like King Saul, are you justifying your disobedience? As you read through this book and study the Word on money, you must answer that question.

The third truth is that *without faith, it is impossible to please God.* I meditated on Hebrews 11:6 for a month and was humbled as God revealed to me how often I don't demonstrate faith in my life. Making decisions without praying for God's direction, worrying over a financial need usually months or years before it will even happen, trying to control a situation for my financial gain, being greedy, and reducing our giving when God has not directed me to do so are all ways that I have not trusted God. Using credit cards that we know we can't pay off at the end of the month or obtaining creative financing so we can have the house we want are just two ways in which we try to take control away from God. I encourage you to write Hebrews 11:6 out on an index card and meditate on it for thirty days. Journal what God reveals to you about your faith.

> *And without faith it is impossible to please Him, for he who comes to God must believe that He is and that He is a rewarder of those who seek Him.*
>
> *Hebrews 11:6*

The final truth is that *earth is not our home; heaven is.* If you have trusted Jesus Christ for the forgiveness of your sins and for eternal life, the Bible tells us that when we die we will be immediately in the presence of God. The Apostle Paul told the church at Corinth that *"to be absent from the body [is] to be at home with the Lord"* (2 Corinthians 5:8). It is also possible that Jesus may return for His saints prior to your death. Either way, you will have very little time on earth compared to your time in heaven for eternity.

Jesus said, *"Do not store up for yourselves treasures on earth, where moth and rust destroy, and where thieves break in and steal. But store up for yourselves treasures in heaven, where neither moth nor rust destroys, and where thieves do not break in or steal"* (Matthew 6:19–20).

Judy and I recently took a trip to Egmont Key, a small island off the coast of St. Petersburg, Florida. In 1898, the United States government made the island into a military base to protect the city during the Spanish-American War. There had been a town of three hundred residents that included a school, YMCA, homes, a Quartermaster's store, and other facilities normally found in a small town. Early in the 1900s, the military closed the base and it began to deteriorate. As we walked around on still-intact streets of what had once been the town, viewing the few remaining partially standing concrete structures, I thought of Matthew 6:19–20. All the temporal things we spend time and money on are going to end up like that military base, while all that we do for the kingdom of God will endure for eternity. We each have a bank account in heaven and on earth. Jesus said that our financial choices on earth will result in deposits in one or the other of these accounts. Which of your accounts has the most treasures?

Are you preparing for heaven or are you being distracted by materialism, work, and busyness? Mark 4:19 says, *"But the worries of the world, and the deceitfulness of riches, and the desires for other things enter in and choke the word, and it becomes unfruitful."* In the Parable of the Talents, the servants that received five and two talents respectively began immediately after receiving their talents to invest and trade them. Their confidence in knowing what their master would want them to do, and knowing who their master was, allowed them to move ahead without fear. Upon his return, their master called them "good and faithful servants." They were prepared not only to be good stewards, but also for the master's return.

My good friend Les Ebert was the Assistant Strength Coach for the NFL Jacksonville Jaguars a few years ago. During one of our visits with him, Les showed me the three-inch-thick manual he had put together, detailing the strength and conditioning plan he would use if he was hired by another NFL team. He had prepared this manual so that when he got a call for an interview for a Head Strength Coach position, he would be ready. Are you as prepared for heaven as Les was for that call from an NFL team?

C. S Lewis wrote, "If you read history you will find that the Christians who did most for the present world were precisely those who thought most of the next. It is since Christians have largely ceased to think of the other world that they have become so ineffective in this."[7] When your focus is on heaven and God, your

---

7 Lewis, C.S. *Mere Christianity* (New York, NY: HarperSanFrancisco, 2001), p. 134.

stewardship of what He has entrusted to you will be for His glory, not yours.

> **Key Point: God's desire is to have our heart, not our offering and sacrifices.**

Cultivating Oneness by Submitting to God's Will

1. What parts of your life have you not given over to God? What is required on your part to do so?

2. Is your account in heaven bigger or smaller than your earthly account? Why?

3. As you memorized and meditated on Hebrews 11:6, what did the Holy Spirit reveal to you?

Additional Resources

Heaven, by Randy Alcorn.

Peggy and I both believe that with God's blessings comes a responsibility to live up to a certain set of stewardship principles. As a husband and wife, we know that we both must affirm these basics or our financial life will be constantly in turmoil. First and foremost is the tithe, which we believe to be the 10% of our gross income which we give to our church home. Offerings are above that and are determined by God's presentation of ministry needs. The tithe is non-negotiable and based on the concept that we are not giving God 10%, but that He is allowing us to keep 90%.

God's ownership of everything is another core belief. With our recognition of God's ownership comes the idea that each purchase we make must not violate who we are in Christ.

While we are not against possessing (stewarding) some nice things, we are careful to make sure that those things do not possess us or in any way damage our witness for Christ. By holding to these core beliefs, we avoid the confrontations about money issues that plague many marriages.

At the end of each month, we sit down and have a "practice spending session" where we allocate all of the income that we expect to receive the following month. The first calculations are easy: tithe, fixed expenses, and those variable expenses that experience has helped us predict. All other expenditures are run through our "God honoring" filter and then assigned to their categories, but we must both agree on the details of the purchase.

This brings two tangible benefits: it limits confrontations over spending and avoids impulse purchases. This kind of systematic agreement over money issues has, through the years, cultivated harmonious decision-making in other areas of our married life, from the raising of children to dealing with in-laws to the allocation of household chores. Once we decided to honor God in our finances, we found ourselves honoring each other in all other things.

—Steve and Peggy Smith
Plant City, FL

Ray Lynch

CHAPTER SEVEN:
THE FINANCIAL PROBLEM

Every man's way is right in his own eyes, but the Lord weighs the hearts.

Proverbs 21:2

The Fall

The first decade of the twenty-first century experienced a number of financial falls, including falling stock markets, falling house prices, and declining pensions and employment opportunities. Former President Ronald Reagan once said that "a rising tide lifts all ships." Also, someone correctly noted during this financially disturbing decade that "a falling tide reveals who is wearing a bathing suit."

This decade was very destructive to many families' finances. There were a record number of foreclosures and bankruptcies during this ten-year period, and in some places there were more houses with mortgage balances greater than their fair market value (FMV) than vice versa. Even with the record number of foreclosures and bankruptcies, which eliminated much debt from many families' financial balance sheets, there was still more debt at the end of the decade than at the beginning. The stress on marriages was unbelievable and many strayed away from their marriages and their faith.

The Symptoms

If your daughter had an internal infection that was causing a high fever and the doctor prescribed two Tylenol and a cold compress, you would surely start looking for another doctor for your daughter. Although the Tylenol and cold compress may briefly help bring down the fever, they would have been of no help for the infection. Left untreated, your daughter may have died.

Just as it's important to treat the medical problem, it's important to treat the financial problem—rather than the symptom. However, more often than not the financial symptom is treated rather than the financial problem.

I believe this is true for two reasons. First, if the symptom is treated instead of the problem, the problem will not go away and the symptoms will come back. By giving us solutions for our financial symptoms instead of our financial problems, the world's financial system will be guaranteed a repeat customer who will have to keep coming back to them for help.

An example of this is a family that refinances their home mortgage and takes out more than is needed so that they can also pay off credit card debt (a financial symptom). During the 1990–2005 period, many homeowners used their appreciating home as an ATM, only to be exposed as not having a bathing suit on when the tide went out. The other option the world offered was home equity lines of credit (HELOCs), which ended in the same manner for the homeowner. In many cases, families ended up having more credit card debt, as well as a higher mortgage or HELOC, because they didn't treat the financial problem causing the credit card debt.

The second reason why the symptom is treated is because that's what many people want. We are living in the day of quick fixes; for example, we take pills to lower cholesterol rather than changing our diets and exercising. I've met too many couples that want their credit card debt to go away quickly (either though refinancing or HELOCs) rather than come up with a budget that reduces spending so that credit cards can be paid off over the next four to five years.

So, the world obliges.

Financial symptoms can be classified into one of three categories: physical, emotional, and spiritual. Below is a list of common symptoms by category.

Physical	**Emotional**	**Spiritual**
Divorce	Arguments	Reduced prayer time
Health issues	Fear of creditor calls	Reduced giving
Loss of job	Stress	Reduced church attendance
Bankruptcy	Broken relationships	Reduced service
Consumer debt	Guilt	Falling away
Late payments	Insecurity	Reduced time in the Bible
Foreclosures	Insignificance	Critical spirit

The Problem

Financial problems fall into one of three categories: ignorance, deception, and wrong attitudes. Let's look at each one.

Ignorance. We're not talking about ignorance of the Bible, but rather ignorance of how to properly manage money. Many of my clients tell me that they understand God owns everything and that they are just managers of what has been entrusted to them. They are familiar with the foundational biblical principles about money, but they do not know how to manage their finances on a day-to-day basis. They have never lived on a budget and they've learned little or nothing from their parents about money management. It's difficult to blame the parents, because many of them weren't taught any money management skills, either. This problem has been going on for a number of generations. Keeping a checkbook register or using cash envelopes is totally foreign to them. Technological advances such as debit cards and online banking have, I believe, made matters worse.

If ignorance is your problem, then read a book on budgeting. My book, *Budgeting for the Non-Accountant*, is available through my ministry website, www.lifechangeconcepts.org. There are many other good budgeting books available. You may also need some hands-on help, so ask your church leadership if there's someone who could mentor you in this area. If your church has a financial counseling ministry, they may be able to help you. The Bible warns us that *"a prudent man foresees evil and hides himself, but the simple pass on and are punished"* (Proverbs 22:3, NKJV). Don't ignore this problem and be punished for it later. Get help now.

Deception. Genesis 3:1 tells us, *"Now the serpent was more cunning than any beast of the field which the Lord God had made"* (NKJV). Just as Satan deceived Eve in the garden—*"The serpent said to the woman,*

'You surely will not die!'" (Genesis 3:4)—he is deceiving Christians today. He has confused us about who God is and what God's Word says about finances, blinding us to the consequences of doing things the world's way. Satan is real and is still in the "surely" business today. Surely you will get that pay raise! Surely you will be able to pay off those credit card charges before the 0% offer expires! Surely you don't need to budget! Surely you are doing fine if you can make the monthly payments! Surely you will be blessed, even though you are disobeying God's Word!

In the Parable of the Talents (Matthew 25:14–30), which is about the return of Jesus and the taking home of the saved, two people are represented: the lost person (i.e. the wicked and lazy servant) and the saved person (i.e. the good and faithful servants). In the parable, the wicked slave had a wrong view of his master (i.e. God) that resulted in him making a money management decision that was very upsetting to his master. Instead of going out and investing the talent he had received, he buried it in the ground and left it there until his master returned. When his master confronted him, the slave said, *"Master, I knew you to be a hard man, reaping where you did not sow and gathering where you scattered no seed.* **And I was afraid**, *and went away and hid your talent in the ground"* (Matthew 25:24–25, emphasis added). This servant had a wrong view of his master because he did not know his master (i.e. he was not born again). In the end, he was thrown into *"the outer darkness; in that place there will be weeping and gnashing of teeth [Hell]"* (Matthew 25:30).

Conversely, the other two slaves, who represented the saved, immediately went and traded the talents given to them. They were able to do this because they knew their master, they had studied his ways, and they understood what he wanted done with his money. Many Christians have been deceived by Satan about who God is and are ignorant of what He wants them to do with the resources

He has entrusted to them. This is largely due to the biblical illiteracy of many believers.

In the box below are a list of four deceptions, the wrong money behaviors that they result in, and the truth that overcomes the deception. Deception is always overcome by knowing the truth. *"So Jesus was saying to those Jews who had believed Him, 'If you continue in My word, then you are truly disciples of Mine; and you will know the truth, and the truth will make you free'"* (John 8:31–32). It is every believer's personal responsibility to study the Bible so that they can know God and His plan for their lives.

Deception	**Wrong Behavior**	**Truth**
1. God is *not* all-knowing. Even if He is, He doesn't sweat the small stuff.	I can disobey God's Word on money and have an abundant life.	*"As obedient children, do not be conformed to the former lusts which were yours in your ignorance, but like the Holy One who called you, be holy yourselves also in all your behavior."* (1 Peter 1:14–15)
2. God is *not* all-powerful. Anyway, He doesn't care about my pain.	My situation is hopeless. I just need to give up. (Bankruptcy, divorce)	*"For nothing will be impossible with God."* (Luke 1:37)
3. God doesn't love me, because I'm a bad person.	I'll buy love. I'll find love in shopping, eating, drinking, and sex.	*"But God demonstrates His own love toward us, in that while we were yet sinners, Christ died for us."* (Romans 5:8)
4. God cannot be trusted. He doesn't keep His promises.	God won't provide if I give to Him first. I need a new car that won't leave me stranded.	*"If we are faithless, He remains faithful, for He cannot deny Himself."* (2 Timothy 2:13)

If deception is your problem, get into a Bible study on the attributes of God, commit to reading through the Bible in one year, and begin memorizing Bible verses.

Wrong Attitudes. Wrong attitudes lead to wrong behaviors. *"For as he thinks within himself, so is he"* (Proverbs 23:7). Our behavior is the result of our thinking. Again, money is not a problem in and of itself. It is the attitude we assume about money and financial matters that may be the problem.

All of us have ungodly attitudes about money, because we are all sinners. Romans 3:23 says, *"For all have sinned and fall short of the glory of God."* We are not born contented beings. Watching a room of playing two-year olds trying to get each other's toys should convince you that we are born with a covetous attitude, not a contented one. The same is true with the other ungodly attitudes about money we will look at in a minute.

If you have placed your trust in Jesus Christ for the forgiveness of your sins, and thus have been born again, you have the Holy Spirit dwelling in you. *"Therefore if anyone is in Christ, he is a new creature; the old things passed away; behold, new things have come"* (2 Corinthians 5:17). You are a new creation with the power to overcome your ungodly attitudes through the light of the Word. *"And He died for all, so that they who live might no longer live for themselves, but for Him who died and rose again on their behalf"* (2 Corinthians 5:15). The way we think about money should result in us living for Christ, not ourselves.

Our churches are filled with Christians who have secular worldviews of money and finances. These are usually people who spend little time studying God's Word. Instead, they accept the messages they receive from the world and other Christians who are handling their finances like the world does. In Chapters Ten through Fourteen, I will share what God says about each of the options we have for using God's money: giving, saving, spending, paying taxes, and incurring and repaying debt. My prayer is that God's truths will result in changed attitudes about money and possessions.

There are far too many ungodly attitudes than this book can cover, but the following are the most common:

Pride

Proverbs 16:18 says, *"Pride goes before destruction, and a haughty spirit before stumbling."* Pride has resulted in many people buying bigger homes than they need, more expensive cars than they can afford, and going out to lunch every day with co-workers rather than admitting that they can't afford it. Pride keeps people from seeking Christian financial counseling. Pride results in parents spending money they don't have in order to keep their children equipped with all the same toys their friends have. Pride prevents us from telling a spouse or child that we are sorry when we have sinned against them.

Pride is ugly! Pride was my biggest ungodly attitude when I was saved in 1986. Shortly after accepting Jesus as my Lord and Savior, God began to humble me in every part of my life. I have come a long way, but the mere memories of some of my prideful acts are still painful to me. My pride led me to lease a minivan in the mid-1990s just before my children came for their summer visit. Our current minivan was in major need of help: the A/C wasn't working, the engine was leaking oil, and the passenger side power window was broken in the partially-down position. In short, it looked just like the eleven-year-old van that it was. All of these ailments made it easy for me to justify leasing a new van.

Like so many other folks who lease, we didn't have any money for a down payment to buy a vehicle. After strong-arming my wife into agreeing with me, we leased the van, but God knew my heart and the ugly pride that was the driving force behind the decision. The sad thing about this story, and millions of similar stories, is that we missed "God's best." By "best," I don't necessarily mean receiving a nicer van. While God surely could have blessed us materially, His best could have been merely helping me to defeat pride in my life.

In addition, how do you think me forcing Judy to agree to buy the minivan helped our relationship? By not even listening to her thoughts, I was signaling to her that I didn't value her or her thoughts. A marriage where one spouse frequently minimizes the thoughts and ideas of the other will ultimately self-destruct. Fortunately, in this case, I had built up a large amount of goodwill through the proper handling of finances in our marriage and our oneness was not seriously damaged.

Humility is the godly attitude we should have. The Apostle Paul wrote in Philippians 2:5 that we should *"have this attitude [humility] in yourselves which was also in Christ Jesus."* His humility resulted in Him obediently dying on the cross for our sins. Verse 9 then says, *"For this reason also, God highly exalted Him, and bestowed on Him the name which is above every name."*

If being more like Jesus doesn't motivate you to be more humble, then let me appeal to your more carnal side with the following promises from God's Word. *"Humble yourselves in the presence of the Lord, and He will exalt you"* (James 4:10). *"The reward of humility and the fear of the Lord are riches, honor and life"* (Proverbs 22:4). What a contrast. The world says that if you operate with power and pride, you will obtain riches. God says that humility brings "riches, honor, and life."

Self-Indulgence

Self-indulgence is a rampant attitude in our materialistic society. In the Parable of the Rich Fool, Jesus describes the self-indulgent person:

> *And he thought within himself, saying, "What shall I do, since I have no room to store my crops?" So he said, "I will do this: I will pull down my barns and build greater, and there I will store all my crops and my goods. And I will say to my soul, 'Soul, you have many goods laid up for many years; take your ease; eat, drink, and be merry.'"*
>
> *Luke 12:17–19, NKJV*

Self was his focus. Jesus called him a fool because he stored up treasures for himself rather than for God.

A number of years ago, when we had our custom drapery workroom, one of our clients paraded out ten winter coats he had recently purchased from L.L. Bean. It seems that he couldn't decide which color he liked best, so he bought one of each. My wife later commented to me how sad it was that many children who attended our church through our bus ministry didn't even have one adequate winter coat to wear, while this man had ten! Like the rich fool, this man had stored up treasures for himself. You may not have ten winter coats, but having just two could still be self-indulgent if God only wanted you to have one.

We should embody the godly attitude of self-sacrifice. Jesus is once again our example. He gave himself for our good. Jesus said, *"For whoever wishes to save his life will lose it; but whoever loses his life for My sake will find it"* (Matthew 16:25).

Fear

Many don't normally associate fear with money problems, and yet it is one of the top two ungodly attitudes, in my opinion. Fear keeps us from trusting God. The writer of Hebrews wrote about God's view on us not trusting Him: *"And without faith it is impossible to please Him (God), for he who comes to God must believe that He is, and that He is a rewarder of those who diligently seek Him"* (Hebrews 11:6). Fear is also the primary attitude driving some people to take total control of the family finances, refusing to allow their spouse to participate.

Here is a partial list of financial decisions I have seen counselees make over the past twenty-two years that were based on fear:

- Fear that they won't be able to get by for the month if they give to God first… so they don't.

- Fear for their children's and their own safety if they do not have cell phones, so they purchase them even though they can't afford them.

- Fear for their safety on the highway unless they are driving a big vehicle, so they trade in their five-year-old car, which they still owe money on, and purchase a new vehicle with a six-year loan which includes the unpaid balance of the previous vehicle and costs them over $500 per month.

- Fear that their job will be eliminated, so they use $40,000 in student loans to get a degree in another profession and $75,000 of credit card debt to survive until school is completed. Two years later, this couple filed for bankruptcy.

- Fear that they will not have enough savings for retirement, so they invest in high-yield, high-risk investments. They lost over seventy percent of their savings when the dot-com bubble burst.

- Fear of missing out on buying a house in 2005, so they purchase a home at the market peak with no money down and an adjustable rate mortgage. They foreclosed in 2009.

- Fear that there isn't enough money to pay the bills… so they don't open them.

All of us make decisions that demonstrate a lack of faith in our all-powerful, all-loving, sovereign God. Examine your financial decisions and honestly appraise how many of them were driven by fear. 2 Timothy 1:7 says, *"For God has not given us a spirit of timidity, but of power and love and discipline."*

Trust is the godly attitude we should have. The more time we devote to Bible study and scripture memorization/meditation, the more God-trusting we become. Isaiah 26:3 says, *"You will keep in perfect peace him whose mind is steadfast, because he trusts in you"* (NIV).

In Chapter Ten, I will share a wonderful story about a Gentile widow who overcame her fear and lived a victorious life of trusting in God.

Covetousness

Like a kid in a candy shop, we want what we can't have. Coveting is wanting more than what God has provided. It results in taking matters into our own hands and not waiting on the Lord and His provision. We are able to live a lifestyle ten to fifteen percent above

God's provision by using debt to pay for our additional spending. I will talk more about debt in Chapter Fourteen.

I have continually seen unsatisfied desires destroys marriages, as one spouse drives the family further and further into debt. King Solomon wrote of the folly of never being satisfied: *"He who loves money will not be satisfied with money, nor he who loves abundance with its income"* (Ecclesiastes 5:10). If you are not content with what God is giving you now, you will not be content when He has given you more. As you read in Chapter Three, discontentment (or covetousness) can be very destructive to the marriage relationship.

We should embrace the godly attitude of contentment. A spirit and attitude of contentment is learned. The Apostle Paul wrote in Philippians 4:11, *"Not that I speak from want, for I have learned to be content in whatever circumstances I am."* Too many of us pray for the Lord to give us enough *money* to live the way we want to live. Instead, we should pray for God to give us enough *faith* to live the way He wants us to live. God cares more about our character than He cares about our comfort. Chapter Twelve discusses contentment in more detail.

Greed

Greed, like the other ungodly attitudes, will result in people taking unreasonable chances with God's money. Every dot-com bubble or housing bubble—really, any kind of bubble—is created by greed. Adding the ungodly attitude of laziness to the mix is a formula for disaster. The belief that one can make a lot of money in a short period of time with little effort is contrary to the Word of God. Yet Christians play the lottery everyday, invest in the latest "hot" stock, and sign up for the latest multi-level marketing scheme that promises the moon. Some Christians even sue other Christians if it promises a big settlement. But Proverbs 28:22 warns that *"A man with an evil eye hastens after wealth and does not know that want will come upon him."*

The husband of one couple that came for counseling had the problem of greed. He had purchased a business he knew nothing about with over $45,000 in credit card debt. His greedy heart left him little time to plan and seek godly counsel before he pulled the trigger on the deal. The result was a failed business and a mountain of debt. In counseling, I pointed out this ungodly attitude of greed, but he never saw it as sin. Therefore, within two years he was involved in the housing boom of 2002–2006. He got into the market early enough to purchase two viable rentals. But greed wouldn't allow him to stop. The purchase of additional rental properties was paid for from the rising equity in the first two houses, which resulted in the foreclosure of all his properties when the market crashed in 2007.

How serious is this sinful attitude? The Apostle Paul says in Colossians 3:5 that greed is idolatry, or the worship of something other than God—*"Therefore consider the members of your earthly body as dead to immorality, impurity, passion, evil desire, and* **greed***, which amounts to idolatry"* (Colossians 3:5, emphasis added).

Generosity is the godly attitude we should have. Proverbs 21:26 says, *"All day long he is craving [greedy], while the righteous gives and does not hold back."* Do you want to stop greediness in its tracks? Then start giving. I discuss giving at greater length in Chapter Ten, but suffice it to say that becoming a joyful giver is more helpful to you than it is to God.

Additional ungodly attitudes and their contrasting godly attitudes are listed below, along with some Bible verses for you to meditate on.

Ungodly Attitudes	Godly Attitudes
Denial (Proverbs 28:19)	Awareness (Proverbs 1:7)
Love of Money (1 Timothy 6:10, Ecclesiastes 5:10)	Love of God (Matthew 22:37–38)
Disobedience (Luke 16:11–12)	Obedience (John 14:21, 1 John 5:3)
Lack of Discipline (Proverbs 25:28)	Self-Control (Galatians 5:22–23)
Laziness (Proverbs 18:9, 19:15)	Diligence (Proverbs 27:23, 1 Corinthians 10:31)
Thanklessness (Luke 17:11–18)	Thankfulness (Philippians 4:6, 1 Thessalonians 5:18)

All ungodly attitudes are sins and are not to be dismissed with an offhand, "That's just the way I am." God never expected us to remain the way we were once we were born again. Ephesians 2:10 says, *"For we are His workmanship, created in Christ Jesus for good works, which God prepared beforehand so that we **would walk in them**"* (author's emphasis). Prideful, greedy, lazy, fearful Christians will not complete the tasks God has prepared for them unless they conform to the image of Christ.

> *Therefore, putting aside all filthiness and all that remains of wickedness, in humility receive the word implanted, which is able to save your souls. But prove yourselves doers of the word, and not merely hearers who delude themselves. For if anyone is a hearer of the word and not a doer, he is like a man who looks at his natural face in a mirror; for once he has looked at himself and gone away, he has immediately forgotten what kind of person he was. But one who looks intently at the perfect law, the law of liberty, and abides by it, not having become a forgetful hearer but but and effectual doer, this man will be blessed in what he does.*
>
> *James 1:21–25*

God does not want us to go through life as defeated Christians, but instead to be victorious. In the next chapter, I show you how you can overcome your wrong attitudes and live a victorious life.

> **Key Point: Failure to address the financial problems creating your negative financial symptoms will result in a wasted life.**

Cultivating Oneness by Identifying and Resolving Your Financial Problems

With your spouse, complete the following activities:

1. List your financial symptoms.

2. What are your financial problems? List your specific ungodly attitudes about money and share an example of when it resulted in a financial decision. Ask God and your spouse for forgiveness for these ungodly attitudes and then, with your spouse, begin to develop a plan to change these attitudes and create safeguards to prevent them from damaging the family's finances.

Additional Resources

Crown Financial Ministry Resources (for more information, see www.crown.org).

CHAPTER EIGHT:
OVERCOMING OUR WRONG
ATTITUDES ABOUT MONEY

I can do all things through Him who strengthens me.

Philippians 4:13

In Chapter Seven, I discussed some of the more prevalent ungodly attitudes about money. These ungodly attitudes are sins which must be dealt with if we are to mature in our faith and have oneness in our marriage through finances. In this chapter, I will discuss three ways for you to achieve victory over these sins: confession, memorization and meditation on God's Word, and choosing to avoid those circumstances which feed your wrong attitudes.

Confession

The first thing we must do with any sin we are attempting to overcome is to confess it to God and ask for His forgiveness and help. 1 John 1:9 says, *"If we confess our sins, He is faithful and righteous to forgive us our sins and to cleanse us from all unrighteousness."* The word "confess" means "to agree with." In agreeing with God that our worldly attitudes about money are sins, we are not only forgiven, but cleansed. We are freed from guilt, which often hinders the overcoming process. Chapter Four discussed this discipline in greater detail.

Too often, we attempt to justify our attitudes ("I'm just like my mother" or "I'm too old to change") rather than confess them. Proverbs 21:2 says, *"Every man's way is right in his own eyes, but the Lord weighs the hearts."* We can fool others and ourselves, but we cannot fool God. So, confess your sinful attitudes as the Holy Spirit points them out to you, and begin to trust an omnipotent God to give you victory in overcoming them.

> While the blood of Christ will cleanse us from every
> sin, it will not cleanse us of even one excuse.[8]

Memorization and Meditation on God's Word

I don't want to trivialize the worldly attitudes you have about money, attitudes which you have taken a lifetime to develop, by saying that you can change them overnight. However, just as I have encouraged you to go to the Word of God for direction in managing the resources He has entrusted to you, we can look to the Bible for guidance on how to overcome our wrong attitudes.

The Lord spoke to the prophet Zechariah, saying, *"Not by might nor by power, but by My Spirit"* (Zechariah 4:6). God has given each born again believer the Holy Spirit to be our Guide into all the truth—*"But when He, the Spirit of truth, comes, He will guide you into all the truth"* (John 16:13). If we try to change our attitudes in our own might and power, the effort will probably end poorly. Remember,

---

[8] Willmington, Dr. H.L. *Willmington's Guide to the Bible* (Carol Stream, IN: Tyndale House, 1984), p. 356.

the Spirit will guide us into all truth and Jesus told us that the truth will set us free.

It is very clear that God wants us to mature and grow in the Lord. He has given us the Spirit to guide us. He puts us through trials to mature us (see James 1:2–4), He chastises us *"that we may share His holiness"* (Hebrews 12:10), and He is at work perfecting us *"until the day of Christ Jesus"* (Philippians 1:6). God does not want us to go through this life continually sinning (which is what our wrong attitudes lead us to) in the way we handle His money, thereby suffering the heavy burdens that these sins bring on our lives. He wants us to have an abundant life of peace, joy, and contentment—right now (see John 10:10).

Finally, He left us His Word. Hebrews 4:12 says, *"For the word of God is living and active and sharper than any two-edged sword, and piercing as far as the division of soul and spirit, of both joints and marrow, and able to judge the thoughts and intentions of the heart."* The Bible is living and active, not just words on a page, because of the Holy Spirit dwelling in us. In Joshua 1:8 God tells us what to do with this living word: *"This book of the law shall not depart from your mouth, but you shall meditate on it day and night, so that you may be careful to do according to all that is written in it; for then you will make your way prosperous, and then you will have success."*

Notice the progression. First meditate on God's Word continually. As you think on the God-breathed words of scripture, you begin to think like God. Then, because you are thinking like God, you start obeying Him. And finally, out of your obedience comes success.

God told the Israelites in the desert that their obedience to His commandments would result in blessings (see Deuteronomy 28:1–14) and their disobedience would result in curses (see Deuteronomy 28:15–45). The curses that result from disobedience are not like the curse God placed Satan under in Genesis 3:14 (*"Because you have done this, cursed are you more than all cattle..."*); instead they are more like a burden. Imagine having to carry one hundred pounds of rocks on your back every waking and sleeping moment of your life. Isn't that how many Christians feel today because they are disobedient to God's Word in how they manage His resources.

God tells us that His living Word can change us. Psalm 119:11 says, *"I have hidden your word in my heart that I might not sin against you"* (NIV). Proverbs 4:23 says, *"Above all else, guard your heart, for it is the wellspring of life"* (NIV). So, God will work through His Word and the Holy Spirit to bring our hearts to a place where we handle the issues of life in accordance with His will.

My Personal Testimony of the Power of God's Word

In 1989, just three years after I was saved, I experienced the power of God. Before I share what happened that day, let me first provide some background. One year earlier, Judy, who I was engaged to at the time, had surgery. Prior to the surgery, a godly lady in our church gave her Isaiah 41:10 to comfort her. The verse says, *"Do not fear, for I am with you; do not anxiously look about you, for I am your God. I will strengthen you, surely I will help you, surely I will uphold you with My righteous right hand."* Even typing out this verse twenty-one years later gives me goose bumps.

Judy and I both memorized that verse before her surgery, and in doing so we were greatly comforted. However, unbeknownst to me at the time, this verse would later help me to cast out fear again. One day in 1989, I was driving somewhere when I began to worry terribly about something. To this day, I can't remember what it was, but I do remember that my fear and worry reached maximum altitude. I literally felt the presence of demons in the car with me. At that moment, the Holy Spirit brought Isaiah 41:10 to mind. Knowing that demons cannot read one's mind and remembering that Jesus had spoken the word to Satan as he tried to tempt Him three times after His forty days in the desert, I quickly spoke the verse aloud. Instantly, and I mean instantly, my worry and fear vanished and an incredible peace came over me. Was it my might and power? Absolutely not! It was the power of God's Word that chased those demons away and brought peace to me. James wrote, *"Submit therefore to God. Resist the devil and he will flee from you"* (James 4:7).

Are you submitting to God and His Word? Do you even know God's Word as it pertains to finances? If not, chapters Nine through Fourteen will give you a great start. Are you reading God's Word daily and memorizing the scriptures? If you spend more time watching the evening news than reading and studying the Bible, there's a good chance that you've flipped James 4:7 around in your life and are now submitting to the devil and resisting God. This, my friend, is not a good place to be.

Our Own Choices

The third thing we can do to overcome our wrong attitudes is to avoid those circumstances that feed our wrong attitudes. Proverbs 22:3 says, "The prudent sees the evil and hides himself, but the naïve go on, and are punished for it." Just as a recovering alcoholic should not go into a bar with friends for lunch, a person who struggles with impulsiveness should not go to the mall with a pocketbook full of credit cards. Nor should a person who struggles with discontentment watch too many Home and Garden TV shows.

If you struggle with:

- Fear, stop watching the nightly news.

- Pride, submit to monthly accountability of your finances with a trusted friend or a trained Christian financial counselor.

- Self-indulgence, give away something in your life (such as clothing) that you have overindulged yourself with.

- Greed, adopt an orphan (or two or three) through www.worldhelp.org, or another Christian child sponsorship ministry.

- Impulsiveness or a lack of discipline, confess your sin to a close Christian friend and ask them to go with you when you go shopping and to hold you accountable if you start to spend without prayer and thought. Or take only the amount of cash you need to buy what you have gone to the store for and leave your credit cards at home

- Laziness, ask your spouse for a list of things you can do for them.

Quite frankly, attempting to break ungodly attitudes in this manner without doing the first two disciplines probably won't last for long, because you would be doing it in your own strength. Therefore, it's important that you implement all three disciplines.

Key Point: Out of His love for us, God has provided all the resources necessary to allow us to have victory over our wrong attitudes about money. The only thing needed is our desire to do so.

Cultivating Oneness through Confession and Scripture Memorization

1. Confess to God and your spouse the sinful attitudes that you identified in Chapter Seven. Your confession must acknowledge that these sins have hurt your family (because they have). Be specific.

2. Ask your spouse to start memorizing scripture with you. Start with one or two verses each week. At the end of each week, recite your new verse as well as the previous verses you have memorized. The Navigators ministry[9] teaches a simple way to memorize scripture: write the verse on an index card and, while looking at it, read it out loud five times in the morning and five times in the evening. By the sixth or seventh day of the week, you will have it memorized. The next week, as you are memorizing a new verse, say the previous verses a couple of times in the morning and evening. Continuing to recite a verse for five to six weeks will lock that verse in your mind for a long time. The reason this technique works is that it involves multiple senses (sight and hearing) as well as muscle memorization. Just as a baseball player teaches his muscles how to field a ground ball by taking a hundred ground balls every day, each of us can teach the muscles around our mouths to memorize scripture. After five or six weeks, take a few weeks off just to work on the verses you have already memorized, then start again with some new verses.

---

[9] For more information, go to www.navigators.org.

3. Ask your spouse to give you some practical ideas to help you avoid those circumstances that feed your wrong attitudes. Listen to them, thank them, and implement their suggestions. This approach not only provides you with healthy ideas, but also lets your spouse know that their thoughts are worthy. In doing so, you are building oneness in your marriage!

Additional Resources

Disciplines of a Godly Man (for Men), by R. Kent Hughes.

Disciplines of a Godly Woman (for Women), by Barbara Hughes.

Ray Lynch

CHAPTER NINE:
THE CHOICE

But as for me and my house, we will serve the Lord.

Joshua 24:15

True Love

Apart from Jesus dying on the cross for our sins, I believe that the greatest demonstration of God's love for us was His willingness to give us free will, or choice. If God had made man without free will and instead programmed us to do only His will, there would have been no sin. Without sin, there would have been no need for the Lamb of God. Without the Lamb of God, we could not know unconditional love. Without knowing unconditional love, we could not know God, for God is agape love.

Compare the parent who controls everything their child does to the parent who allows their child more and more freedom to choose as they grow towards adulthood, thus allowing them at times to fail. Who is expressing love? Free will allows us to experience true love.

Free will gives us the freedom to choose the gift of forgiveness from God, to forgive our spouse when they wrong us, to yield to the Holy Spirit, to manage God's money His way, to be intimate with our spouse, to live on a budget, to not fall into debt, and to cultivate oneness in our marriage. We also have the freedom to do none of these things.

But contrary to the beliefs of many, our choices do have consequences. A look at two hearts and two choices of two men in the Old Testament confirms this.

Two Men, Two Hearts

The story of Abram and his nephew, Lot (found in Genesis 13:1–13) is a great illustration of man's freedom to choose and the consequences of choosing the world's way instead of God's way. In Chapter Seven, you learned how the heart (attitude) leads to habit (action).

As the story unfolds, we see that Abram and Lot have returned from a stay in Egypt, where they accumulated great wealth. However, this great wealth caused problems, just as it has always done throughout the ages. Genesis 13:7 tell us that *"there was strife between the herdsmen of Abram's livestock and the herdsmen of Lot's livestock."*

Verse 4 has already given us a glimpse into Abram's heart, where we read, *"And there Abram called on the name of the Lord."* When Abram responds to this strife, we see the impact that walking with God has on how we handle God's money and possessions. First, Abram was the one to bring up the problem. Second, he sought to be a peacemaker rather than benefit from the situation, as he said, *"Please let there be no strife between you and me..."* (Genesis 13:8). Third, even though Abram was the senior person in this circumstance, he offered Lot the choice of where he wanted to live. It's important to understand that in their culture the older person was considered the wisest and most revered. Abram could easily have pulled rank and told Lot where to move. Instead he demonstrated great humility.

Lot, on the other hand, showed the condition of his heart by taking Abram up on his offer. Understanding his position in this relationship, he should have said, "I greatly appreciate your generous offer, Uncle Abram, but as your humble and lowly nephew I must request that you choose where I should go." Instead, Lot wasted little time after the offer. *"Lot lifted up his eyes and saw all the valley of the Jordan, that it was well watered everywhere"* (Genesis 13:10).

In the next verse, we see that *"Lot **chose** for himself **all** the valley of the Jordan"* (Genesis 13:11, emphasis added). What a contrast there was between these two men. Abram was God-focused, a peacemaker, humble, and generous. Lot was greedy, selfish, and disrespectful.

How did Lot make his choice? What did he base his decision on? Lot made this extremely important decision based on what he could see— *"Lot lifted up his **eyes and saw** all the valley of the Jordan, that it was **well watered everywhere**"* (Genesis 13:10, emphasis added). The Bible gives no indication that Lot consulted with the Lord, and he certainly didn't consider the spiritual ramifications of his decision. We know this because of what happens next. Lot chose for his family to move to Sodom, where the men were *"wicked exceedingly and sinners against the Lord"* (Genesis 13:13). Do you think he was going to find a good church for his family in Sodom? Sadly, he didn't even factor this into the decision-making process.

Lot was thinking temporally regarding his finances instead of eternally. He chose the world's way rather than God's way. As Randy Alcorn says in his book, *Money, Possessions and Eternity*, "The key to our use of money and possessions is having the right perspective—an eternal perspective."[10] Abram had the right perspective, but Lot did not.

The Apostle Paul wrote to the Christians in the church of Corinth on this same subject:

> *Therefore we do not lose heart, but though our outer man is decaying, yet our inner man is being renewed day by day. For momentary, light affliction is producing for us an eternal weight of glory far beyond all comparison, while we look not at the things which are seen, but at the things which are not seen; for the things which are seen are temporal, but the things which are not seen are eternal.*
>
> *2 Corinthians 4:16–18*

What do you measure your financial decisions by? Are you considering the eternal factor in your decisions on how you manage God's money?

Do you honestly desire God's way for your life by searching the scriptures, praying fervently to God, and seeking godly counsel? Are you prideful or humble, greedy or generous, selfish or selfless in making your financial decisions? Are you more like Lot or Abram?

If you have been more like Lot, then I hope a look at the rest of Lot's life will convince you that you are on a road to destruction. After five more chapters devoted to the life of Abram, we arrive at Genesis 19, where we learn of the consequences of choosing the world's way of handling finances over God's way. God destroyed Sodom. Since Lot and his family had become well-integrated into this immoral city, they suffered also.

The Bible says, *"Lot was sitting in the gate of Sodom"* (Genesis 19:1), which is where the commerce of the city took place. In verse 8, Lot

---

[10] Alcorn, Randy. *Money, Possessions and Eternity* (Wheaton, IL: Tyndale House, 2003), p. 451.

offered his daughters to the lust-filled men of the city. Later, after realizing the danger they were in, Lot tried to persuade his sons-in-law to leave with them, *"but he appeared to his sons-in-law to be jesting"* (Genesis 19:14). The consequences were terrible. As Lot's family fled the city, they were commanded to not look back. *"But his wife, from behind him, looked back, and she became a pillar of salt"* (Genesis 19:26).

In the end, Lot's wife and sons-in-law died while he and his two daughters escaped only because of God's mercy. The chapter ends with total humiliation as his daughters get him drunk and have intercourse with him. Lot lost everything: his family, his integrity, his investments, his home… everything.

Lot did not sit down years earlier when Abram offered him the chance to choose and say, "My goal for five or ten years from now is to have my wife and sons-in-law die, lose all my investments, and impregnate my two daughters." None of the people who lost their homes when the housing bubble burst in America in 2006 accounted for as part of their five-year plan, yet it happened anyway, because they didn't follow God's principles on money.

Handling God's money and possessions the world's way is no laughing matter. I have counseled hundreds of men and women who have experienced broken relationships and financial destruction because they did things the world's way. In Chapters Ten through Fourteen, I will tell you what God says about giving, saving, family needs, taxes, and debt… and also remind you what the world says. God wants us to be good and faithful with everything we have, because it is all His. My prayer is that you will be a doer of the word—not just a hearer.

But in the end, the choice is yours.

The Mind of Christ

Although God has placed us in an environment that is hostile to His ways, He has not left us alone. What a great God! He has given us the Holy Spirit. Jesus said:

> *I will ask the Father, and He will give you another Helper, that He may be with you forever; that is the Spirit of truth, whom the world cannot receive, because it does not see Him or know Him, but you know Him because He abides with you and will be in you.*
>
> *John 14:16–17*

The Apostle Paul told the Corinthian believers that *"we **have** the mind of Christ"* (1 Corinthians 2:16), which allows us to *"know the things freely given to us by God"* (1 Corinthians 2:12). Ephesians 2:10 says, *"For we are His workmanship, created in Christ Jesus for good works, which God prepared beforehand so that we would walk in them."* Philippians 1:6 says, *"For I am confident of this very thing, that He who began a good work in you [your salvation] will perfect it until the day of Christ Jesus."* Philippians 4:13 says, *"I can do all things through Him who strengthens me."*

God has equipped us to discern the correct choices and the power to make the correct choices. If you are having a difficult time understanding God's Word—or worse yet, have little or no desire to read and study God's Word—you have continued in a pattern of ungodliness with regards to money and other parts of your life. You must seriously question whether or not you have been born again. I'm not trying to put you on a guilt trip, but just because you said a prayer at some point in your life doesn't mean you are born again.

The Apostle John wrote the following: *"By this we **know** that we have come to know Him [Jesus], if we keep His commandments. The one who says, 'I have come to know Him,' and does not keep His commandments, is a* *liar, and the truth is not in him"* (1 John 2:3–4, emphasis added). When you said that prayer, did you truly believe in your heart that you are a sinner, that Jesus is God the Messiah, and that He died for your sins and was raised from the dead? If you are trusting in anything other than the shed blood of Jesus for your salvation, you need to get together with God right now and *"confess with your mouth Jesus as Lord"* (Romans 10:9). When you have been born again, you will *know* it!

> **Key Point: Our financial choices have consequences, either positive or negative.**

Cultivating Oneness by Choosing God's Way

Discuss the following questions with your spouse now and again after reading Chapters Ten through Fourteen.

1. Think back to your most recent financial decision (such as a vacation, the purchase of a car or house, or the choice of a job). Did you demonstrate humility or pride, selflessness or selfishness?

2. When God reveals a truth to you, do you then obey that truth or continue to disobey?

3. Do you measure financial decisions by their impact on God's kingdom work or on the impact of your bottom line?

4. We have five places where God's money can go—giving, saving, spending, paying taxes, and repaying debt. Trying to determine how the money God has entrusted to us should be allocated (making

115

choices) creates tension between each of the choices. How much should go to giving, savings, and spending? Limiting one category creates more for the other categories, and vice versa. As we go through different seasons of our lives, the allocations can change. Do you feel this tension? If you do, try to explain it to your spouse. If you don't, check back to this question after you have read Chapters Ten through Fourteen.

Additional Resources

Money, Possessions and Eternity, by Randy Alcorn.

We were doing great. We owned our own business and were flipping houses, something we both had dreamed about for years. Then the market crashed… and we crashed with it. Our finances were turned upside-down and we quickly ran out of money. After many months of looking for work, Dan finally landed a job that would at least work for us temporarily. But that's when it really hit us. What were we going to do about our late bills? Our mortgage, our credit cards, our utilities… we were behind on everything. We could feel our marriage suffering because of the stress this was bringing into our lives.

We were going in opposite directions when it came to our money. That's when we were referred to LCC, and we are forever grateful. First and foremost, we realized that we needed to pray together for guidance and wisdom about our finances. With the guidance of LCC, we implemented a budget, and more importantly we stuck to it. We started to sit down every month to look at our budget and have open communication about any concerns. Instead of just giving an offering at church, we started to tithe. Things were so much better.

About three months ago, Dan got another job. This time, it's a lot closer to his ideal job, although we would need to move three hours away. Because we had been living on a budget for the last two years, it was so much easier to sit down and talk about how we could work things out financially, praying together for direction.

We have now made the move and feel blessed by the new job. In times like these, we are reminded that God is at the center of our marriage and He will guide us in all *things… including our finances.*

—Dan and Tina Stumpfhauser
Bonita Springs, FL

Ray Lynch

CHAPTER TEN:
GIVING

For if there is first a willing mind, it is accepted according to what one has, and not according to what he does not have.

2 Corinthians 8:12 (NKJV)

Matthew 6:21 says, *"For where your treasure is, there your heart will be also."* Financial stewardship has everything to do with our heart and attitudes towards money and possessions. Therefore, as we look at each area where God's money goes, we'll look at these choices from a heart perspective.

Grace Giving

Many people teach that the Bible commands us to give ten percent (the tithe) of our income. The church I was saved through, and every church I have been a member of since, has taken this position. Other Bible scholars believe that the tithe is not a part of New Testament giving. There are sound arguments on both sides of the tithe issue. However, for the purpose of this book, it's not necessary to enter into this debate. Jesus and the Apostle Paul, who was the largest contributor to the New Testament, had ample opportunity to resolve the tithing issue, but neither did so. Instead both focused on giving with the right heart. I will also. We will call this grace giving. Even if you don't believe the tithe is commanded for today, you're not released from giving, particularly because of limited income.

Both the story of the widow's mite (see Mark 12:41–44) and the way Paul shared of the generosity of the Macedonian churches of who were in deep poverty (see 2 Corinthians 8:1–5) indicate that no level of income should preclude us from giving. New Testament writings demonstrate that everyone is to be involved in giving. The tithe, whether applicable to the New Testament or not, at least supports the belief that every Christian should be giving.

How much should we give? One of the problems I have with the tithe teaching is that it gives some who do tithe (by giving ten percent of their income) a false sense of assurance that they are giving as they should be. However, New Testament giving should outpace Old Testament giving, because the truth of God's salvation plan has been fully revealed to us. We have full knowledge of what perfect giving is: Jesus dying for our sins so that we can be reconciled to God through faith. Becoming more Christ-like requires us to be more giving. Paul explained very clearly in 2 Corinthians 9:6–13 that our giving should not plateau at a level such as the tithe, but should continue to grow as God provides abundantly. The only thing that should plateau is our spending, which will be discussed further in Chapter Twelve. Some believers, such as Rick Warren and the late Bill Bright, understand this principle and give significant portions of their incomes to kingdom work.

Pastor Skinner, who led me to the Lord, always said that we can never out-give God. This is a true statement for two reasons. First, no matter how much we give, it can never reach the benchmark that Jesus set. Second, no matter how much we give (with the correct heart), God will always create more from it, multiplying our seed for sowing and increasing the harvest of our righteousness (see 2 Corinthians 9:10).

Throughout the New Testament, the emphasis is on the motive (heart) for giving rather than the amount given. An incorrect motive led to the death of Ananias and Sapphira (see Acts 5:1–11), while Paul urged each Corinthian to give *"just as he has purposed in his heart, not grudgingly or under compulsion"* (2 Corinthians 9:7). Gracious giving is a reflection of the grace God showered on us through His Son's sacrifice for our sin. When we give graciously, it demonstrates our love for Jesus and shows our recognition of what He did for us (see 2 Corinthians 8:9). Paul says, *"I am not speaking this [their pledge to give to the church in Jerusalem] as a command, but as proving through the earnestness of others the sincerity of your love also"* (2 Corinthians 8:8). Paul later says that their giving was proof of their love (see 2 Corinthians 8:24).

Our giving is a reflection of our *trust* in God and our *love* for Him. As our trust in and love for God deepens, our giving *will* increase. A Christian cannot grow spiritually if he gives sparingly. Such giving leads to a self-centered life rather than a Christ-dependent one.

The Trusting Gentile Widow

There are two Bible stories involving single women that demonstrate how *trust* and *love* impact our giving. The first is found in 1 Kings:

> *Then the word of the Lord came to him [Elijah] saying, "Arise, go to Zarephath, which belongs to Sidon, and stay*

there; behold, I have commanded a widow there to provide for you."

So he arose and went to Zarephath, and when he came to the gate of the city, behold, a widow was there gathering sticks; and he called to her and said, "Please get me a little water in a jar, that I may drink."

As she was going to get it, he called to her and said, "Please bring me a piece of bread in your hand."

But she said, "As the Lord your God lives, I have no bread, only a handful of flour in the bowl and a little oil in the jar; and behold, I am gathering a few sticks that I may go in and prepare for me and my son, that we may eat it and die."

Then Elijah said to her, "Do not fear; go, do as you have said, but make me a little bread cake from it first and bring it out to me, and afterward you may make one for yourself and for your son. For thus says the Lord God of Israel, 'The bowl of flour shall not be exhausted, nor shall the jar of oil be empty, until the day that the Lord sends rain on the face of the earth.'"

So she went and did according to the word of Elijah, and she and he and her household ate for many days. The bowl of flour was not exhausted nor did the jar of oil become empty, according to the word of the Lord which He spoke through Elijah.

1 Kings 17:8–16, emphasis added

Before reviewing this story, it is important to provide a brief background. Elijah was the prophet of Israel and Israel was suffering through a horrible drought that had led to a famine in the land. Economically speaking, times were very hard. The two players in this story are Elijah and a widow with a son.

We pick up the story in verse 8, where God commands Elijah to go to Zarephath and meet up with a widow who will provide for him. Verse 8 also tells us another very important fact: God has also spoken to the widow and has commanded her to provide for Elijah.

When Elijah arrives, he asks the widow for a drink of water. She immediately sets out to get the water, but Elijah stops her and asks her for a piece of bread. From her reaction to these two requests, I believe we can draw the following conclusion: water was available to her, but bread was not. She said *"As the Lord your God lives, I have no bread, only a handful of flour in the bowl and a little oil in the jar; and behold, I am gathering a few sticks that I may go in and prepare for me and my son, that we may eat it and die"* (1 Kings 17:12). She had no problem getting Elijah water, but when he asked for bread, of which she only had a little, she broke down. The Bible doesn't say, but she probably poured out these words as tears ran down her cheeks.

In Chapter Seven, I talked about the need to correct our financial problems rather than our symptoms. The widow's financial symptoms were that she was very depressed to the point of giving up all hope and her lack of food. What financial problem was causing these symptoms? Some might say the famine or the fact that she was a widow in a culture where such a condition could be financially debilitating. It was none of these. Just as we pointed out in Chapter Two, God knew this widow's problem and He pointed it out to her through Elijah. In verse 13, Elijah said to her, *"Do not fear."* Her problem was fear and her lack of trust in God was causing her depression and lack of food.

Remember that God spoke to the widow in verse 8 and commanded her to provide for Elijah. Would God have done that without providing for her to do so? The answer is an emphatic NO! Where God guides, He provides. The widow knew what God was telling her to do, but she did not trust Him. She allowed her circumstances to guide her actions and attitudes. Too often, we do the same thing. Peter did the impossible by walking on water until he took his eyes off Jesus and put them on his circumstances (Matthew 14:28–33).

In the widow's defense, it should be pointed out that she was a Gentile who did not believe in the God of Israel. In verse 12, she responds to Elijah's request for bread by saying, *"As the Lord your God lives…"* (emphasis added). This was Elijah's God, not hers; at least, not at this point.

Trusting God During My Unemployment

In 1991, I lost my job on a Friday. By the next Monday, ten well-meaning Christian brothers and sisters had reminded my wife and me that I needed to apply for unemployment compensation. Quite frankly, until the first person said something, neither of us had thought of this. Strangely, as people began to mention it to us, we both became more and more uneasy with the prospect. We continued to pray for God's direction over a period of one week, but as more and more people urged me to file, I began to accept their counsel.

Judy still did not have a peace, so I suggested that we call Larry Burkett's live radio finance show for counsel. In my heart I knew that Larry would say file for the unemployment. Well, Judy got through and I listened on the radio upstairs as he told her it was okay to take the unemployment compensation. She was very saddened by his counsel, sensing that, even though it was okay to take, we were going against the Holy Spirit's prompting. I felt the same way but did not let on to her that I did.

The next day, I drove to the unemployment office and arrived about twenty minutes before opening. I had taken my Bible with me and began reading where I had left off in Exodus.

As I was reading, God spoke to me in that still small voice. He said, "Read Matthew 6:24."

My response was that I knew the verses in Matthew 6.

The still small voice came back, "Not Matthew 6:25-34 (God was reading my mind again), but Matthew 6:24."

So I turned to Matthew 6:24 and read, *"No one can serve two masters; for either he will hate the one and love the other, or he will be devoted to one and despise the other. You cannot serve God and wealth."*

As the Holy Spirit began to bring tears to my eyes, God said, "Ray, I created the universe in six days; don't you think I can provide for you during the next six months?" That was the length of the unemployment compensation.

At this point in the conversation I was crying uncontrollably. God had made His point and all I had to do was start the car and drive home.

On the way home, I told God that I was going to keep a record of every extra dollar that He provided over and above the income from my wife's business. I did this not because I didn't believe God, but because I did believe Him and wanted to have proof for other less trusting Christians. When I shared with Judy my conversation with God, we both rejoiced and praised God. For the first time since the layoff, we were at peace.

The point of this story is not to say that unemployment compensation is wrong, but that when God is telling you to do something, obey Him, regardless of what others are saying.

God's Promises

The widow of Zarephath was confronted with a word from God just as my wife and I were. How would she respond? In His grace, God took this untrusting widow in His arms and through Elijah restated His promise: *"For thus says the Lord God of Israel, 'The bowl of flour shall not be exhausted, nor shall the jar of oil be empty, until the day that the Lord sends rain on the face of the earth'"* (1 Kings 17:14). God was reminding her that where He guides, He provides.

What does this have to do with Christians today? God has made the same promise to us that He made to that widow: where He guides, He provides. God has promised in Matthew 6:33, Philippians 4:19, 2 Corinthians 9:6–11, Proverbs 3:9–10, and other verses that He will meet our every need if we are faithful in our stewardship, which includes giving generously.

God's Testing

Does your giving indicate that you are trusting in God or yourself to get you through the month? Interestingly, after Elijah pointed out that her problem was a lack of trust, he went on to say, *"Go, do as you have said, but make me a little bread cake from it **first** and bring it out to me, and afterward you may make one for yourself and for your son"* (1 Kings 17:13, emphasis added).

By requesting that the widow feed him first, Elijah wasn't being uncaring. Instead, God was testing her to see whether a heart change had occurred and she was ready to be a doer of the word, and not just a hearer. After God has revealed a truth from His word to me, He often puts me into a situation, just as He did with the widow, which gives me a chance to obey that truth.

The Victorious Widow

We see her response in verse 15: *"So she went and did according to the word of Elijah."* This Gentile woman, who moments earlier had given up on life because she did not trust Elijah's God, obeyed Him. This is a real woman with whom we will spend an eternity. Where are you today? Are you married and struggling to trust God with your pocketbook, divorced and struggling to get child support, single and trying to pay off college debt, unemployed with little or no income, or maybe widowed like this unnamed women in 1 Kings 17? More than likely, your condition is not as bad as this widow's. Are you ready to embrace God's promises and to trust Him with your giving and your finances? If you do, you will never, ever regret it. After you have examined your spending, develop a budget that allows you to start giving. Then, just as the widow did, experience God as you never have before.

If you're already giving, consider increasing the amount. Maybe you can begin to support a missionary or an orphan through an organization like World Help or Compassion International. This second suggestion is great if you have children. You can teach them a lot about being generous by allowing them to give from their allowance or earnings to support a child. In addition, they can write letters to your sponsored child.

The Loving Sinner

The second Bible story, found in Luke 7:36–47, gives us a beautiful picture of how our love for Christ impacts our giving.

> *Now one of the Pharisees was requesting Him [Jesus] to dine with him, and He entered the Pharisee's house and reclined at the table. And there was a woman in the city who was a*

sinner; and when she learned that He was reclining at the table in the Pharisee's house, she brought an alabaster vial of perfume, and standing behind Him at His feet, weeping, she began to wet His feet with her tears, and kept wiping them with the hair of her head, and kissing His feet and anointing them with the perfume.

Now when the Pharisee who had invited Him saw this, he said to himself, "If this man were a prophet He would know who and what sort of person this woman is who is touching Him, that she is a sinner."

And Jesus answered him, "Simon, I have something to say to you."

And he replied, "Say it, Teacher."

"As a moneylender had two debtors: one owed five hundred denarii, and the other fifty. When they were unable to repay, he graciously forgave them both. So which of them will love him more?"

Simon answered and said, "I suppose the one whom he forgave more."

And He said to him, "You have judged correctly." Turning toward the woman, He said to Simon, "Do you see this woman? I entered your house; you gave Me no water for My feet, but she has wet My feet with her tears and have wiped them with her hair. You gave Me no kiss; but she, since the time I came in, has not ceased to kiss My feet. You did not anoint My head with oil, but she anointed My feet with perfume. For this reason I say to you, her sins, which are many, have been forgiven, for she loved much; but he who is forgiven little, loves little."

Luke 7:36–47

This story (also recorded in the other gospels: Matthew 26:6–13, Mark 14:3–9, and John 12:1–8) is about an immoral woman who anointed the feet of Jesus with a very expensive perfume, probably worth about one year's worth of wages, while He was having dinner at the home of Simon, a Pharisee. This woman's action brought a negative response from the others who were at the dinner, both from Simon, who was also a leper, and the disciples of Jesus. Simon could not understand why Jesus allowed this immoral woman to touch Him. In the other gospel accounts, the writers said that even the disciples of Jesus were indignant when they saw what she had done. They thought her to be wasteful. Obviously, she was not a crowd pleaser or follower of the hypocritical religious rules of the day. Instead, she was a follower of her heart and her heart loved Jesus. When you give generously out of love, you, too, will have many people, including Christians, think you are crazy.

In response to Simon's concern, Jesus shared a story about two debtors: one who owed five hundred denarii, and the other fifty. When they were unable to repay, the moneylender graciously forgave them both. Jesus then asked *"Which of them will love him [the moneylender] more?"* (Luke 7:42)

Simon correctly answered, *"I suppose the one whom he forgave more"* (Luke 7:43). Jesus then pointed out to Simon that he had not cleaned His feet when He arrived, which was the custom of the day, while this woman had cleaned His feet with her tears and anointed them with perfume. In contrast, Simon, the leper, who was an outcast because of his disease, had showed little gratitude to Jesus for befriending him.

Jesus then concluded by saying that *"her sins, which are many, have been forgiven, for she loved much; but he who is forgiven little, loves little"* (Luke 7:47). Jesus was showing the contrast between Simon's heart and the woman's heart. Simon considered himself righteous and in need of only a little forgiveness.

In this story, the woman is representative of all Christians. Jesus was the substitute for the penalty we should all have had to pay for our sins. When you understand how needy you are for Christ, you understand the magnitude of what Jesus did for you and me, the price He paid and what we received (see 2 Corinthians 8:9). This woman understood.

I suggest you take some time to read the gospel accounts of Jesus' death and remember that you will be spending an eternity with God, not because of anything you did, but because He willingly died on the cross and paid our sin penalty (see Romans 6:23). As this truth becomes more real to you, I believe your future giving will come out of a heart of worship and love rather than compulsion, and that it will be as generous as that redeemed woman in the story.

Key Point: Where we allocate God's money is where our heart and devotion will be.

Cultivating Oneness In Your Giving

My wife and I are in perfect agreement regarding our giving. We have always thankfully given more than ten percent, as we were taught to tithe as young Christians. If you and your spouse are not in agreement on giving, there are some options. For example, if the husband does not want to give, the wife should ask if he would agree to her giving a portion of her own earned income. If he says no, then submit to his position and begin to pray for God to change his heart. If the wife does not want to give, the husband should ask her if there is a level of giving she would be comfortable with, that would make her feel secure. Whatever that amount is, that is what they should give. Then he should begin praying for her faith to grow and for her security to be in Christ.

To cultivate oneness in giving, it's more important to show love and respect for your spouse than to drag them out of where they are in their faith walk. God knows your desire to give, but He would much prefer a great marriage. If He can change the heart of a king, He can certainly change your spouse's heart regarding giving. Let Him do the heavy lifting.

> If our expenditures on comfort, luxuries, amusements, etc., is up to the standard common among those with the same income as our own, we are probably giving away too little. If our charities do not at all pinch or hamper us, I should say they are too small.[11]

> *Do not store up for yourselves treasures on earth, where moth and rust destroy, and where thieves break in and steal. But store up for yourselves treasures in heaven, where neither moth nor rust destroys, and where thieves do not break in or steal; for where your treasure is, there your heart will be also.*
>
> *Matthew 6:19–21*

You can't take it with you, but you can send it ahead. Which of your bank accounts has more in it—your bank account in heaven or on earth?

When was the last time you and your spouse prayed about how much and where you would give? If it has been a long time, each of you should take two weeks to pray about how much you will give

---

[11] Lewis, C.S. *Mere Christianity* (New York, NY: HarperSanFrancisco, 2001), p. 86.

to your church. Each of you can write on an index card the amount God has placed on your heart. Compare the numbers at the end of two weeks and go with the number you can both agree on, whether it be the higher or lower number or an average of the two numbers.

Additional Resources

Generous Living, by Ron Blue.

God Owns My Business, by Stanley Tam.

My wife Amy and I have been what I consider to be good financial stewards. We've always budgeted, tithed, and prayed over making major financial decisions. For me personally, financial stewardship has been the strongest part of my Christian walk.

During the first five years of our marriage, Amy and I were blessed tremendously in the area of finances. We both worked full-time and had no children, minimal debt, and few expenses. Nor did we have any expensive tastes. My primary business was commercial real estate and business boomed from 2004 to 2006. In 2006, we had our first child and Amy stopped working to become a stay-at-home mother. In 2007, my income began a drastic downward spiral with the collapse of the real estate bubble. For the next three and half years, we watched our income level significantly decline as well as our savings. Now, in mid-2010, we have three kids and a family of five living off thirty percent of the income we had when it was just Amy and me.

During the good times, we were in agreement to never live beyond our means, but in fact to save, knowing that the good times would not last forever. As such, we are able to take shelter during the harsh economic downturn. The Lord blessed us with great timing as we began building our home, pre-boom, in late 2002. We put down fifty percent to keep our mortgage payment low and resisted the temptation to refinance and pull out most of our equity during the boom.

As a result of our faithful stewardship, God has blessed us so that we are able to give more than our ten percent tithe. Amy and I have always been unified in our willingness and desire to give to others in need—often anonymously. A few years back, some friends of ours were in need of marital counseling yet lacked the finances to afford the cost. Amy and I prayerfully decided to donate the cost of their counseling directly to the church without telling our friends. They received the necessary counseling, for the betterment of their marriage, under the guise of a scholarship.

We continue to be blessed, even during these difficult times, because our financial struggles have brought us closer to one another and closer to God. In the past, we seldom discussed finances, as Amy just deferred to me to make all the financial decisions and to set our budget. Amy and I now talk almost weekly about our finances as we discuss the previous week's purchases while mapping out the next week's financial plan.

—Bill and Amy Renje
Tampa, FL

CHAPTER ELEVEN: SAVING

Go to the ant, O sluggard, observe her ways and be wise, which, having no chief, officer or ruler, prepares her food in the summer and gathers her provision in the harvest.

Proverbs 6:6–8

What Is Not Saving

A man's wife returns home from a wonderful day of shopping and excitedly proclaims that she saved fifty dollars because she bought a one hundred dollar dress that was marked down by fifty percent. Her frugal husband quickly reminds her that she had not saved fifty dollars, but instead *spent* fifty dollars. Retailers market their products in a way that helps the buyer feel good about spending money. They do this by using words like "saving," "discounts," and "everyday low prices," which put a positive spin on spending.

Now, I'm not saying that all spending is bad, but buying things you don't need because they are on sale is a problem. This is one of many misconceptions of what saving is. The following are some others:

- Believing that having fifty dollars from each paycheck direct-deposited into your savings account so that you can later withdraw it to pay bills is saving.

- Believing that the equity that's accumulating in your home because of rising house prices is saving.

- Believing that credit cards are your emergency savings.

What Is Saving?

To save means to set aside a reserve of money. The Bible tells us that the wise person saves, while the fool doesn't. *"There is precious treasure and oil in the dwelling of the wise, but a foolish man swallows it up"* (Proverbs 21:20).

When I was growing up, my parents repeatedly told my sister and me to spend less money than we made. They reinforced this idea by giving me a dime bank that was shaped like a cash register when I was ten years old. After I had put in ten dollars' worth of dimes, a little door in the back would open and all one hundred dimes would fall out. By the time I had saved my first ten dollars, my parents had already taken me to the bank to open a savings account, so I would have a place to deposit my ten dollars.

My parents grew up during the Great Depression, so saving was a high priority to them. Prior to the Great Recession, which we are currently in as of the writing of this book, most Americans had not experienced the financial pain that my parents did and thus didn't see the urgency of saving. Hopefully the pain many have and are experiencing from the Great Recession will raise the importance of saving to its rightful position, just behind giving. Anyway, the availability of credit cards has given many people a false security about being prepared for that "rainy day" that comes to all of us.

Why Save?

The Bible tells us that there are three reasons we should be saving. The first is for the proverbial rainy day. Just as Egypt suffered through seven years of famine during Joseph's time (see Genesis 41:1–37), world economies go through financial recessions which result in lost jobs. While God warned Egypt of the impending famine, He usually does not give us warning of coming financial setbacks. Thus, the wise person saves for those rainy days. Judy and I were able to get through my job loss in 1991 and her job loss in 2008 without using debt because we had savings.

Most counselors will tell you that you should have three to six months' worth of spending in your rainy day fund. Therefore, if you are spending $5,000 per month, you should have $15,000 to $30,000 in emergency savings. When I share this with most of my counselees, their jaws drop and they ask how this is possible. God's Word gives us the answer, and I will share this wisdom with you after giving you the remaining reasons we should be saving.

God does not tell us to save a certain amount, and thus leaves room for Himself to be God in our lives. Therefore, if God is telling you to give more during a period of your life, making saving difficult, it does not mean that you are foolish. During difficult periods in our lives, God has challenged Judy and me to give amounts that left little for saving even though we deeply cut our spending. My story in Chapter Twelve about our house on Appling Valley Drive was one of those times. We weren't foolish for not saving during these periods, nor would you be.

The second reason to save is to provide for our family. *"But if anyone does not provide for his own, and especially for those of his household, he has denied the faith and is worse than an unbeliever"* (1 Timothy 5:8). That language is pretty strong! Are you financially prepared to help an adult child who has just lost his job or is struggling with large medical bills, or to have an elderly parent come live with you? Unfortunately, poor saving discipline is often passed down from generation to generation, which makes it difficult for multiple generations of a family to comply with the admonishment of 1 Timothy 5:8.

One gentleman shared with me that he ran up $30,000 in credit card debt helping his son and daughter-in-law though a difficult financial situation. I don't think this is what God meant when He told us to provide for our family. I will explain why in Chapter Fourteen.

Providing for our households also includes saving for the next car, the roof replacement, the college tuition, and retirement. Are you getting a picture as to why you should be saving ten to fifteen percent of your income on a regular basis? If you say that's not possible, then you have created a lifestyle that is outside God's will and you must begin to downsize. Chapters Eleven and Fourteen through Eighteen will help you to do this.

Before I go to the last reason for saving, I want to share a warning about saving for the family. Many couples in their twenties and thirties, who understand the wisdom of saving, put too much emphasis on saving for retirement. They will put ten to fifteen percent of their income into their 401K accounts while saving little for the down payment for their first home or for the rainy day. These couples usually end up using credit cards to supplement their income, particularly when the first child comes along. Build a solid foundation of a fully-funded rainy day account and money for at least a ten percent house down payment before putting large amounts towards retirement.

The third reason to save is so you can help others. Ephesians 4:28 says, *"Let him who stole steal no longer, but rather let him labor, working with his hands what is good, that he may have something to give him who has need"* (NKJV). 2 Corinthians 8:14 says, *"...but by an equality, that now at this time your abundance may supply their lack, that their abundance also may supply your lack—that there may be equality"* (NKJV). How did those Corinthian Christians have so much to share? They were savers. If you think about it, all of your savings will ultimately either be given away or spent.

During our search for a church shortly after moving to Tampa in 1998, Judy and I attended a Sunday evening service devoted to a missionary couple blessing us through song. At the end of the service, the church elder who was leading the service announced that the couple's RV was in need of repair and that they didn't have the funds to pay for it. To our shock, the elder didn't take an offering but instead just asked for prayer. Immediately, I felt the tug of the Holy Spirit, telling me to go up to the couple and ask how much they needed. After they informed me that they needed $800 for the repair, I told them that I needed to speak with my wife. I felt led to give them the full amount, but I knew this would be God's will only if He was telling her the same thing. I told Judy of the need and asked her thoughts (oneness is asking and listening, not telling). She said that the Lord was telling her that we should cover the whole repair even as I was going up to the couple. That gift came out of our savings.

How to Save

Earlier, I mentioned how shocked many counselees are when I tell them how much they should have in their rainy day fund, and how quickly they respond to the impossibility of that happening. The Bible tells us that it is possible, and there are millions of families that can give personal testimony to that truth. Proverbs 13:11 says, *"Dishonest money dwindles away, but he who gathers money little by little makes it grow"* (NIV).

We are called to give an honest day's work. *"He who is slothful in his work is a brother to him who is a great destroyer"* (Proverbs 18:9, NKJV) Surfing the internet on company time, taking company supplies home for personal use, lying to a perspective customer about your product's capabilities in order to make a sale, and playing the lotto are all ways to accumulate dishonest money. But living a life of integrity and spending less than God gives you will result in large savings.

Putting a mere $200 per month into a savings account earning two percent annually for sixty months, or the length of many car loans, will net you approximately $12,500 in savings. When your $400 per month car payment is done, drive the car for another five years and put the $400 in savings. Even at the two percent rate of return, you would have over $25,000! Start looking today for that $200 or $400 per month that you could wisely put into savings.

Saving Too Much

Someone once said, "A miser isn't any fun to live with, but he makes a wonderful ancestor." Over-saving at the expense of giving to God, building relationships, and loving your neighbor is a foolish thing to do.

Jesus spoke of such a man in Luke 12:13–21. A rich farmer, who had been enormously blessed by God, chose to build bigger barns and retire—*"And I will say to my soul, 'Soul, you have many goods laid up for many years to come; take your ease, eat, drink and be merry'"* (Luke 12:19). Jesus said that he was a fool because he had stored up treasures for himself and was not rich toward God.

When you're saving more than you are giving, you're probably on thin ice. A sure way to avoid being a hoarder is to be rich toward God in your giving.

> **Key Point: A prudent man saves; a wise man knows when to stop.**

Cultivating Oneness with Your Savings

My wife and I track our income and expenses on a monthly basis, and because of that we both know how much we are saving. At the end of each year, we update our net worth using a form found on my ministry website, ww.lifechangeconcepts.org. We also review our retirement accounts and other investments together, discussing how they are impacted by our planned budget for the coming year. To be honest, my wife cares little about our investments, but we take the time to do this because she needs to have this knowledge for when we have financial decisions to make, or in the event that I die. I cherish her input on all financial issues and don't want her handicapped during that process by her lack of knowledge.

We *never* go forward with any financial decision of significance unless we are of one spirit and mind. For years, I would talk about buying a house as an investment property and Judy would quickly say no. She understood that neither of us was cut out to be landlords, regardless of how good the investment was financially. I didn't go off and pout like some husbands do when they don't get what they want—or worse yet, go ahead with the plan without her consent. I've heard countless stories from wives about their husbands purchasing jet skis, boats, and other toys without them being onboard (no pun intended).

After numerous suggestions and rejections over the years about buying a rental property, our good friend Bill Renje came to me one day with an offer to participate in the purchase of an apartment building. Bill was a commercial realtor who specialized in the small- to medium-size apartment market, so when he said that this was a very good deal, I believed that it was something we should be involved in. Bill is a godly man who also happened to be very good at what he did, so I trusted his analysis. I told him I would discuss the deal with Judy and get back with him, the whole time thinking of all those rejections Judy had made of previous efforts to get into the rental business. Much to my surprise, when I presented the offer to her she said she was open to praying about it. To make a long story short, she had peace about the investment and we went ahead with it. At this writing, it has turned out to be the best investment we've made in a long time.

Ephesians 4:1–3 says, *"Walk in a manner worthy of the calling with which you have been called, with all humility and gentleness, with patience, showing tolerance for one another in love, being diligent to preserve the unity of the Spirit in the bond of peace."* Follow these three verses and you won't have any problem cultivating oneness with your finances.

1. Individually, list five things you can do to free up $300 per month for saving, then compare and discuss with your spouse. While your spouse is explaining how they would reduce spending by $300 per month, *listen!* When one is done, let the other speak. How many of the spending cuts were for things *you alone* use or enjoy?

2. If you have school age children who are considering college, brainstorm ways that they could complete college without student loans.

3. Does your employer offer a 401K retirement program that you are not participating in? What would need to happen in order for you to begin contributing at least one percent of your income to it?

If one of you is the homemaker or is self-employed, is the family budget allowing that spouse to contribute to an IRA?

Additional Resource

Austin Pryor's Christian Financial Newsletter (www.soundmindinvesting.com)

Ray Lynch

CHAPTER TWELVE:
SPENDING

For what is a man profited if he gains the whole world, and loses or forfeits himself?

Luke 9:25

Henry David Thoreau said, "Almost any man knows how to earn money, but not one in a million knows how to spend it." He must have lived in a neighborhood with a lot of politicians in order to be so pessimistic! I'm a little more optimistic than Mr. Thoreau. However, he did hit the nail on the head when he observed that negative financial symptoms are almost always due to overspending rather than too little income. To say you don't have enough money is to say that God, who promises to meet all our needs, has not done so.

The problem is not that God doesn't know our needs, but that *we* don't know our needs! In order to sell their products and services, companies, through marketing and advertising, have convinced many people that their *wants* are really *needs.* Many companies that produce products for the well-to-do—like BMW, Ethan Allen, and others—through shrewd marketing have convinced many less affluent families that they, too, should and could have their products. Debt has made an affluent lifestyle available to middle class families who have been deceived by marketers.

Growing up in Milford, a small farming community in Delaware, you could tell everyone's financial status by the car they drove. The doctor or attorney drove the Cadillac while the factory worker drove a Chevy. Back then, people didn't have six-year car loans, so they tended to buy what they could afford. Today, with leases and six-year loans, people with a beer budget and champagne taste can drive a car that only an executive could afford sixty years ago.

My Needs, Your Wants

In our materialistic society, where everyone is trying to keep up with their neighbor or brother-in-law, we have missed an important point: what is a *need* for one person may be a *want* for someone else. Although some may need an SUV or a four-bedroom, three-thousand-square-foot house, we don't all need them. I have found that the people who live a lifestyle closest to that of their actual needs are the people who are successful financial stewards. For example, I have met a number of generous givers and wise savers who are also great relationship builders.

As you begin to develop your budget, which will hopefully conform to God's will, match it up with the biblical principles found in the Bible as outlined in this and other Bible-based finance books. As you evaluate your lifestyle against the Bible, as opposed to popular marketing, you will be able to discern what the needs truly are for your life.

146

To help you in this process, let's define what a need and a want are. *Needs* are our basic requirements necessary for living: food, shelter, clothing, and transportation. For instance, in the 1950s, a typical family with three children would only need a three-bedroom, two-bathroom, thirteen-hundred-square-foot home. As technologies advance and societies change, however, a person's needs may change. For instance, the introduction of the internet into our society has created a legitimate need for many to have a computer, whereas twenty years ago this need did not even exist.

Wants are choices about quality and quantity of goods to be used. For instance, a family may need only a cell phone for Dad and Mom, making additional phones for the children a want.

To illustrate how one person's need is another person's want, take the following quiz. First, identify which of the following items you currently have in your life by putting a check in the box next to each item. Then go back and mark whether those items you identified as being in your lifestyle are truly a need or a want by circling either the N or W.

❑ 60-inch flat screen TV   N or W _____

❑ 42-inch regular TV   N or W _____

❑ Cable TV (more than the basic)   N or W _____

❑ Cable TV with only local channels   N or W _____

❑ 4-bedroom/3-bath house   N or W _____

❑ 3-bedroom/1-bath house   N or W _____

❑ New SUV   N or W _____

❑ 8-year-old 4-door sedan   N or W _____

- [ ] iPhone   N or W _____
- [ ] 3 or more computers in your home   N or W _____
- [ ] 3–5 work lunches out per week.   N or W _____
- [ ] Take lunch to work 5 days per week   N or W _____
- [ ] Eyeglasses   N or W _____
- [ ] Contact lenses   N or W _____
- [ ] Invisible bifocals   N or W _____

Now, in the far right blank space, check each item that could be in your life if you lived in a small village in a rural part of Kenya, where there's no electricity, running water, gas stations, or paved roads and you, like the other residents of the village, are a farmer.

The purpose of this exercise is twofold: first, to help you see how many wants you already have in your life, and second, to validate the fact that one person's needs are not another person's needs. I'm incredibly thankful to God for being an American citizen and having access to an abundant lifestyle that's shared by less than ten percent of the world's population. But it is because there is so much available to me that I must be ever-diligent to remember what items are really needs for my life.

I'm not saying that we should void ourselves of all wants in our lives. Jesus even said in Matthew 6:33 that if we *"seek first His kingdom and His righteousness, [then] all these things will be added to you."* In the Greek, "added to you" means to give you abundantly over what is needed. God promises that if we are keeping Him and His kingdom first in our lives, He will bless us. If we are truly managing God's money and possessions with the belief that He is sovereign and in control, and if we believe that without faith it is impossible to please Him, and that heaven, not earth, is our home (see Chapter Six), we will not see the abundance as being for us, but instead for kingdom work.

> *Your needs will never get you in trouble – it's the wants that get you into trouble.*
>
> *—Anonymous*

Counselees over the years have tried to get me to tell them how they should spend God's money. However, because God primarily gave us principles for managing money instead of commands, and because needs and wants are different for everyone, I explain to them that God, not Ray, needs to direct them to the correct lifestyle. In addition to giving them foundational truths to guide them, I also share three other biblical principles that, if applied to the spending part of their budget, will help them to create a lifestyle that conforms to God's will for them. These principles are: *learn* to be content, put God first and *live* expecting His provision, and *love* correctly.

Learn to Be Content

> *But godliness actually is a means of great gain when accompanied by contentment. For we have brought nothing into the world, so we cannot take anything out of it either. If we have food and covering, with these we shall be content.*
>
> 1 Timothy 6:6–8

The story is told of a farmer who lived on the same farm all his life. It was a good farm, but the farmer began to tire of it with the passing years. He longed for a change, for something "better." Every day he found a new reason to criticize the old place.

Finally, he decided to list the farm with a real estate agent, who promptly prepared a sales advertisement. As one might expect, the advertisement emphasized all the farm's positives: ideal location, modern equipment, healthy stock, acres of fertile ground, etc. Before placing the ad in the newspaper, the realtor called the farmer and read the copy to him for his approval. When he finished, the farmer cried out, "Hold everything! I've changed my mind. I'm not going to sell. I've been looking for a place like that all my life!" The farmer had become discontented because he focused on what the farm did not have rather than what it did have. Marketers bombard us daily with hundreds of messages that shift our focus to what we do not have, rather than what we do have. As a result, like the farmer, we, too, become discontented.

The Apostle Paul wrote in Philippians 4:11, *"Not that I speak from want, for I have* **learned** *to be content in whatever circumstances I am"* (emphasis added). We must each learn to be content, because we are born with a sinful heart that makes coveting more natural than being content.

So, how do we learn to be content? By focusing on the foundational truths I discussed in Chapter Six—everything is God's and He is in control of who gets what. Paul wrote in Philippians 4:19, *"My God will supply all your needs according to His riches in glory in Christ Jesus."* To not be content with what we have today is to not be thankful to God for what He has chosen to give us.

This brings me to the second discipline for learning to be content: continually giving thanks for everything. 1 Thessalonians 5:18 says, *"In everything give thanks; for this is God's will for you in Christ Jesus."* God understands that when we are giving thanks for the things in our life on a continuous basis we won't have time to focus on what we don't have.

The third discipline that helps us to be content is being generous with what God has given us. I have found in my twenty-two years of counseling that the people who give the least are the people who are the most discontented.

In Chapter Three, I wrote about the damage that discontentment can have in a marriage, so applying these three disciplines—of understanding the source of everything we have, giving thanks for everything we have, and finally being generous with everything we have—is vital to creating oneness in your marriage. In addition, as you learn contentment, you will find that your spending will decrease.

In the late 1990s, a group of Americans were asked what they would do for ten million dollars. Seven percent said they would murder for the money, while twenty-five percent would abandon their family and sixteen percent would leave their spouse. This, my friends, is not a picture of a contented nation.

> *A rich person is not the one who has the most, but is the one who needs the least.*
>
> *—Anonymous*

Put God First and Live Expecting His Provision

"But seek first His kingdom and His righteousness, and all these things will be added to you" (Matthew 6:33). This is one of the great promises from God. He tells us that if we seek to glorify Him, He *will* provide our needs. We don't need to worry about tomorrow. But in truth, we often do exert too much time and energy worrying.

James wrote about the double-minded man whose doubting of God's provision made him *"unstable in all his ways"* (James 1:8). This struggle with confidence in God reminds me of the story of the six-year-old boy who, upon being told by his parents that Mommy was going to have a baby, told them that he hoped it would be a baby brother. In fact, he began praying every night with his dad for a baby brother. Around Christmas time, he and his father were at the mall when Dad decided to let his son see Santa. When Santa asked the boy what he wanted for Christmas, he responded, "A baby sister." This perplexed the father, so on the way to the car he asked his son why he'd asked Santa for a baby sister when he had been praying to God for a baby brother. His son quickly replied, "I'm trying to find out who is real!"

We laugh at this story, but this is exactly how a lot of Christians are living today. We say that we trust God for our daily bread, but we quickly use the credit card to purchase things we believe we need, knowing that we won't pay off the balance when the next statement arrives. We don't even factor God into the equation. I often ask counselees how God was involved in their last vehicle purchase, and about ninety-five percent say that they didn't involve Him at all.

As we move towards a Christ-focused and Christ-dependent life, an interesting thing happens: we want less and less of the world's materialism and our spending goes down. Living this life of Christ-dependence is hard, because God does not always provide in the way we want or in the time we expect. Judy will tell you that I am the great planner, and I am too often trying to figure out how God is going to provide. Just as often, God reveals His wonderful creativity by providing in ways that prove beyond a shadow of doubt that it was from Him.

The House on Appling Valley Drive

In October 1993, Judy and I moved from the townhouse we had been renting to a beautiful four-bedroom rental house on about a third of an acre in Fairfax, Virginia. We needed to move because our in-home custom drapery workshop had outgrown our townhouse.

Our new home far exceeded our needs and appeared to be another wonderful gift from God. We were informed by the owner before we signed the lease that they only wanted to rent the house for one year, and then they were going to sell it. When they asked us if we would be interested in buying the home at the end of the year, we explained that it may be difficult for us to get a mortgage since we didn't have a long financial record from the business to show the bank. They replied that they would be happy to finance the loan. Their willingness to finance the mortgage was just one of many factors in this deal that made us feel very confident that this was the house God wanted us to have.

At the time we signed the lease, with an option to buy, we had less than $2,000 in savings. This may surprise you, since earlier I shared that I am a saver. The limited savings wasn't the result of an overindulgent lifestyle, but instead because God had challenged us during this season of our life to be very generous. During this period, our giving was at its greatest percentage of our income. We were putting God first in our giving, as well as all other parts of our lives. In this context, God brought us to this incredible home that was perfect for our business and every aspect of our lives.

Knowing that we would need approximately $20,000 for a down payment in twelve months, Judy and I and a few close friends began to pray for God's provision. We never worried about how we would save $18,000, but made every effort to further reduce spending in order to come up with the money. But God had another plan, one that would glorify Him, not us. As much as we tried during that year to save the additional money, God did not allow our business to produce enough profit to do so (remember, God controls even your business). As a result, we were about forty-five days away from the end of the lease with only $3,000 in savings. We decided at that point to give the owner our answer thirty days before the end of the lease in order to give them some time to market the house in the event we didn't buy it.

Six days before that self-imposed deadline, my unsaved father came to visit us from Florida. The first evening, while sitting together in the family room, my father announced that he was giving us half of the inheritance from his mother's estate. She had died nine months earlier and in her will she had left both my sister and me approximately $43,000 in U.S. savings bonds. At the time of her death, my father, who was the executor of the will, had decided to keep the money in his estate and pass it on to us at the time of his death. However, he informed us that evening that about two months earlier he had felt the need to give each of us exactly half of the inheritance.

I tell you by the authority of God's Word that his change of heart was God hearing our prayers and answering them. When we deducted the ten percent we would give to the Lord and the amount we needed to cover the taxes, we were left with $500 more than we needed for the down payment. God didn't have my father give us the full amount, because we didn't need it. He only gave us half in order to show us beyond a shadow of doubt that He was the One who provided the needed funds. Are you putting God first in your marriage, finances, and other parts of your life? If so, confidently trust that He will be faithful to *"supply all your needs according to His riches in glory in Christ Jesus"* (Philippians 4:19).

> *I have been young and now I am old, yet I have not seen the righteous forsaken or his descendants begging bread.*
>
> *Psalm 37:25*

Love Correctly

What do you love? Most Christians quickly answer, "God, family, and country." Maybe a few will add chocolate to the list! But do our lives support this answer? The rich ruler in Luke 18:18–23 was invited by Jesus to be one of His disciples—to eat, walk, sleep, talk, and study with Jesus. He was invited to have an intimate relationship with the Son of God! But he chose not to. Why? Because of things. That's right, things. He preferred to have his money and material possessions over a close, intimate, personal relationship with his Creator. Many Christians are missing that very same relationship with Christ and with family and neighbors because of *things* in their lives.

Things are bigger houses than we need, houses and yards that must be picture perfect, walk-in closets full of clothes not worn in years, endless activities for the children, every electronic gadget produced, collectibles, investments, etc. Many of our things have been boxed-up and stored away in attics and garages for years. Things hinder our relationships with God, family, and neighbors. Our children have all the latest toys, but little time with their parents. Parents have all their toys, but little time for God.

Mark 4:19 says, *"But the worries of this world, and the deceitfulness of riches, and the desires for other things enter in and choke the word, and it becomes unfruitful."* There's nothing wrong with any of your things, unless you love them more than you love God. How do we know when this is the case? Like in the case of the rich ruler, when you are not willing to give them up. Do you have things in your life that you're clinging to? Things that clutter your day and prevent you from getting to know God, your family, and your neighbors more intimately?

I once met a man who worked three jobs in order to earn enough money to take his family to Disney World for ten days. As a result, he had little time to spend with his wife and three children, and God. Unfortunately, when the time came, he spent his vacation with four strangers.

As you spend more time with God and His Word than you do at the mall, your finances and relationships will get better. Michael Card wrote a song entitled "Things We Leave Behind" that expresses this principle of loving correctly quite well. As you read these words, think about what things in your life are keeping you from true freedom.

> Every heart needs to be set free
> From possessions that hold it so tight,
> 'Cause freedom's not found in the things that we own.
> It's the power to do what is right
>
> With Jesus, our only possession
> And giving becomes our delight
> And we can't imagine the freedom we find
> From the things we leave behind.
>
> We show a love for the world in our lives
> By worshipping goods we possess.
> Jesus has laid all our treasures aside
> And love God above all the rest.
>
> 'Cause when we say no, to the things of the world
> We open our hearts to the love of the Lord and
> It's hard to imagine the freedom we find
> From the things we leave behind.[12]

---

[12] Card, Michael. "Things We Leave Behind." *Poiema*. Mole End Music, 1994.

Only God satisfies. Don't let things get in the way.

—Anonymous

> **Key Point: Materialism binds us to the curse of protecting and maintaining our stuff, while the pursuit of God produces riches without sorrow (see Proverbs 10:22).**

Cultivating Oneness in Your Spending

Judy and I cultivate oneness in the area of spending by first developing together a written budget for the upcoming year (Chapter Sixteen shows you how to create a realistic budget), and then abiding by it to the best of our abilities (Chapter Seventeen discusses how we use cash envelopes to control discretionary spending). We do this by tracking our previous month's spending and income together the first week of every month (Chapter Eighteen discusses these monthly financial reviews).

We do not spend any money that is outside our budget without first discussing it together and praying over the decision. We never move forward with a decision unless we both have peace about it. We each have our allowances for clothing, haircuts, personal items, gifts for each other, and lunch with a friend, which gives us enough autonomy and prevents control issues from popping up.

Ray Lynch

CHAPTER THIRTEEN:
TAXES

However, so that we do not offend them, go to the sea and throw in a hook, and take the first fish that comes up; and when you open its mouth, you will find a shekel. Take that and give it to them for you and Me.

Matthew 17:27

Taxes are seldom discussed when Christians talk about financial stewardship. However, because taxes unfortunately represent a growing portion of what God has entrusted to us, and because it is where we find His only command given on money, I will spend some time examining what God's Word says about it. The good news is that this will be a short chapter!

Jesus commanded us to pay our taxes, and He Himself paid taxes. The command is found in Matthew 22:21, which says, *"Then render to Caesar the things that are Caesar's; and to God the things that are God's."* The point is made again in Romans 13:6–7, which says, *"For because of this you also pay taxes, for rulers are servants of God, devoting themselves to this very thing. Render to all what is due them: tax to whom tax is due..."*

In Matthew 17, a tax collector asks Peter if Jesus will be paying *"the two-drachma tax"* (Matthew 17:24). Jesus instructs Peter to go fishing and tells him that the first fish he catches will have a shekel in its mouth and that he is to use that money to pay the tax. Later, Jesus tells Peter that they are paying the tax *"so that we do not offend them"* (Matthew 17:27). Part of being a good financial steward is paying what we owe in taxes when they are due. It is our responsibility to follow civil laws as part of our submission to government (Romans 13:1–4), which is one of three institutions God established (the other two are the church and the family).

Our Responsibility

Even though our government is making the tax code more and more complicated each year, it is still our responsibility to complete our tax returns and pay what we owe in a timely fashion, so that we do not offend them.

As a tax preparer, unfortunately, I see too many Christians doing a poor job with this portion of their stewardship. Most folks who work for a company as a W-2 employee pay their taxes on time because the government withholds the taxes out of each paycheck. However, some individuals significantly over-withhold, resulting in large refunds (anything over $1,500) when they submit their tax returns. This, in and of itself, would not place you in the category as a bad steward.

What results in poor stewardship is when those who get a large tax refund 1) pay interest charges and late fees throughout the year because they don't have enough monthly income to pay their bills on time, or 2) use much or all of the refund on things that are wasteful or unwise. For instance, I once knew a single mom with two children who used her $2,500 tax refund to take her family on a cruise instead of using it to start an emergency saving fund, which she did not have. Needless to say, when her old vehicle required some significant repair work five months later, she did not have the money.

If you are getting a large refund every year, I recommend that you increase the number of exemptions on your W-4 and begin putting that money into savings, if you don't need it. If you do need it, that may mean that you're current on all your bills and don't need to use credit cards.

Finally, in the interest of cultivating oneness, you and your spouse need to discuss your options and come to an agreement on how the extra money from each paycheck will be used before changing your W-4. If you need to change your W-4, ask your payroll department for a new W-4 to complete.

Taxes for the Self-Employed

If you are self-employed or work as an independent contractor for another company (and receive a Form 1099-MISC), you need to be making quarterly estimated tax payments to the federal and state Departments of Treasury. One mistake that I see all too often is when self-employed individuals fail to make these payments. They tell me that they can't afford to make the payments because they need all the profits from their business for personal needs. I tell them that they either need to grow their profits (by increasing sales and/or reducing business expenses), cut their personal expenses, or find a part-time job to supplement their business income. *Not paying taxes is not an option.*

Too many self-employed people delay the inevitable decision to shut down their business, get a part-time job, or try something else by either not paying their taxes (which results in interest and penalties to the taxing agency) or using credit cards to supplement their income. *Both choices are very bad ideas.*

Record Keeping

Whether you're self-employed or working for someone else as a W-2 employer, keeping your tax-related documents is essential for the accurate and timely completion of your taxes (for the self-employed, this means keeping expense receipts and records of deposits). If you don't know what you're doing in this area, seek out godly counsel. *Ignorance is not an excuse.*

If you are self-employed, having a separate business checking account would be a helpful step towards keeping good business records.

The world's way is:

- to underpay taxes by overstating business expenses or deductions, and/or understating income, or

- to avoid paying taxes altogether by failing to file a return.

The fact that you have a slim chance of getting caught is irrelevant. What is relevant is the fact that we serve an Omnipresent and Omniscient God Who knows everything we do and who desires for us to be holy. So do everything (even your taxes) to the glory of God. 1 Corinthians 10:31 says, *"Whether, then, you eat or drink or whatever you do, do all to the glory of God."*

Cultivating Oneness with Your Taxes

As I said above, I am a tax preparer and, therefore, I do our taxes each year. I must confess that I have often let the busyness of the tax season prevent me from sitting down with Judy and fully explaining our tax return (so writing this book is helping me do better at cultivating oneness, too!). The accuracy of our tax return is a shared legal responsibility, so she needs to be involved even though it is an area where she puts complete trust in me to do what is right.

If you have someone doing your taxes, go to the tax preparer together. If your spouse is doing your taxes, get involved, particularly if either of you are self-employed. I've had too many counselees (mainly divorced women) share about deceit by their ex-husbands in this area, resulting in huge tax liabilities.

Final Points

All income, except gift money, is taxable income and must be reported. Therefore, cash income from a business must be reported. Also, if you do a lot of cash transactions in your business, you need to be sure that you have a paper trail of either an invoice or cash receipt.

If you do your own taxes, you should either use tax software or the IRS site to do so. The tax code is so complicated that doing your taxes by hand will surely result in errors.

> **Key Point: To violate tax laws is to break the only command on money that God gives us.**

Ray Lynch

CHAPTER FOURTEEN:
DEBT

You were bought with a price; do not become slaves of men.
—1 Corinthians 7:23

I once said during a radio message that the credit card is the greatest curse on America in the past fifty years. The use of all types of debt by Christians has modeled the world's way and resulted in incredible heartache and destruction in the American family. No other part of financial stewardship is more misunderstood and misused than debt. I hope this chapter will open your eyes to God's perspective on debt and set you on a new course that will eliminate (or at least reduce) debt in your lives.

The Bible does not clearly tell us that borrowing is a sin, except in the case where one does not repay his debt. Psalm 37:21 says, *"The wicked borrows and does not pay back, but the righteous is gracious and gives."* Does this mean that bankruptcy is a sin? I will answer that question later in this chapter.

Although the Bible does not directly state that borrowing is a sin, aside from Psalm 37:21, God does give us warning signs regarding the use of debt. Just as a person driving on a winding road on a rainy day would react to a diamond-shaped orange sign with wavy parallel lines by slowing down, we should also heed God's biblical warning signs about debt. Let's look at these warning signs and then try to establish a Bible-based strategy for borrowing.

- Whenever the Bible addresses borrowing, it is always in a negative context. One example is found in Deuteronomy 28:43–45, where God tells the Israelites that "the alien among you shall rise above you higher and higher, but you will go down lower and lower. He shall lend to you, but you will not lend to him; he shall be the head, and you will be the tail. So all these curses shall come on you and pursue you and overtake you until you are destroyed, because you would not obey the Lord your God by keeping His commandments and His statutes which He commanded you." In that day, borrowing was a judgment of God for disobedience.

- In addition to being a sign of disobedience, debt also produces bondage. Proverbs 22:7 says, "The rich rules over the poor, and the borrower becomes the lender's slave." Many of the slaves in Jesus' day were slaves because they could not pay back a debt they had incurred. Even though debtors' prison and slavery are limited to a few places around the world today as a threat for failing to repay debt, emotional and spiritual bondage does still exist. The ride up Debt Mountain is filled with fun and frolic, but ultimately the creditors will cut off the debt spigot and end the fun. The stress of being unable to make even the minimum payments on credit card bills, receiving endless calls from collectors, or being two months behind on a car payment and wondering whether your car will be in the driveway when you wake up in the morning, is an emotional drain. I have seen the debris left along the road of life everyday—divorce, high blood pressure, sleepless nights, two jobs and no time with the family—and so have other Christian counselors and medical doctors.

- Debt also presumes upon the future. Proverbs 27:1 says, "Do not boast about tomorrow, for you do not know what a day may bring forth." James 4:13–14 says, "Come now, you who say, 'Today or tomorrow we will go to such and such a city, and spend a year there and engage in business and make a profit.' Yet you do not know what your life will be like tomorrow. You are just a vapor that appears for a little while and then vanishes away." Borrowing presumes that you will be able to make the monthly payment until the debt is paid off. Few people heeded this warning during the go-go years of the housing boom, and as a result they suffered dearly for it. Borrowers usually focus on whether they can make the monthly payment. In the case of buying an automobile, a good salesperson will ask, "How much can you afford a month?" and totally steer the conversation away from the actual purchase price. They will lengthen the loan or maybe reduce the interest rate slightly in order to come up with the monthly payment you can afford. While I'm on the subject, the truth of the matter is that most people really don't even know what monthly payment they can afford because they're not living on a budget and tracking their monthly income and expenses. The longer the length of the loan, the greater your presumption on God's grace. Just because you can make a loan's monthly payment doesn't mean that it's God's will for you to purchase that item.

• Finally, debt pays the creditor financing charges and other fees. The typical American family today has eight credit cards with $9,000 in unpaid balances, two vehicle loans, a student loan, and a mortgage. The total interest they pay monthly is approximately $1,200! Think about what could be done with that money. My wife and I support three orphans through an organization called World Help. It cost $90 per month to feed, clothe, educate, and provide safe shelter for those three kids. One day, as I was praying for our orphans, the thought came to me that there are 180 million orphans around the world, many living in non-Christian environments. What if every one of the sixty million professing American Christian families sponsored three orphans? We could put every orphan in a safe Christian environment where the good news of Jesus Christ could be taught to them. Talk about worldwide evangelism! What would it take—$90 per month? Unfortunately, most of the families paying $1,200 per month in interest cannot do this. Without debt, these families could not only support three orphans, but they could start a college fund for their children, allow the mom to stay at home, or go annually on a memory-making vacation. God said, "Owe nothing to anyone except to love one another; for he who loves his neighbor has fulfilled the law" (Romans 13:8). Being free from debt frees us from interest charges and other fees, allowing us to use these resources to love God, our family, and our neighbors as God would want us to.

If the Word taught me anything, it taught me to have no connection with debt. I could not think that God was poor, that He was short of resources, or unwilling to supply any want of whatever work was really His.[13]

When Is Borrowing a Sin?

Earlier, I said that borrowing and not paying back the debt is a sin (see Psalm 37:21). I believe there are two other cases where borrowing is a sin. The second case in which borrowing is a sin is when debt *prevents a sovereign God from enacting His will in our lives.* For example, God may provide us with what we believe to be inadequate resources at times in our lives in order that He might demonstrate His power to provide for us, either through others (see 2 Corinthians 8:14–15) or Himself (Exodus 16:4–5). Or He may put up financial barriers to prevent us from making certain decisions (such as borrowing to start a business that we are not prepared to manage or that He doesn't want us to be involved in) that would cause us harm. God loves us and knows exactly what is best for us.

The third case in which borrowing would be a sin is when it *promotes sinful attitudes and behaviors,* such as impulsiveness, fear, self-indulgence, covetousness, and pride. Debt allows us to purchase

---

[13] Taylor, Dr. and Mrs. Hudson. *Hudson Taylor's Spiritual Secret* (Chicago, IL: Moody Press, 1989), p. 82. The Taylors were missionaries to China in the 1800s.

more house or car than we need and to live a lifestyle that is inconsistent with God's plan for our lives.

By eliminating credit card debt and car loans, my wife and I have greatly simplified our lives. Think about it: over the past year, how many fewer options would you have had to pray and agonize over if you hadn't had the option of using debt to purchase it? By drawing a line in the sand that says we will not have credit card debt, Judy and I demonstrated that we trusted God's promises (such as the ones Matthew 6:33 and Philippians 4:19).

In 1989, when we started Judy's custom drapery workroom, we did not need to borrow money, nor did we borrow for the next nine years, even though we had to purchase some pretty expensive sewing machines. In 1991, when I lost my job and our income plummeted from $6,000 per month to $1,000 per month, God was faithful to provide for us.

For nearly twenty-two years of marriage we have been faced with the same financial challenges that nearly everyone experiences, yet we have never had credit card debt. God has always been faithful to provide for our needs, and He will do the same for you (a review of Chapters Nine and Eleven may be necessary to put God's promises in the proper context).

Debt is a tool; yes a tool to nail your coffin shut!
—*Anonymous*

Bankruptcy

Earlier, I shared Psalm 37:21, which probably made those who have already filed bankruptcy at some point in their lives a little uneasy. I believe that God is a God of grace. He knows we live in a sin-cursed world and that there will be times when bankruptcy is necessary. After all, God is the one who created the Jubilee Year in the Old Testament (Leviticus 25:8–55).

The Jubilee Year was established, in part, to give people a chance to start over, economically and socially. It reminds us of God's interest in liberty; God wants people to be free (Jesus said in Luke 4:18–19, *"The Spirit of the Lord is upon Me, because He anointed Me to preach the gospel to the poor, He has sent Me to proclaim release to the captives, and recovery of sight to the blind, to set free those who are oppressed, to proclaim the favorable year of the Lord"*). It also stands as a witness to God's desire for justice on earth and calls into question any social practices that lead to permanent bondage and loss of economic opportunity—can anyone say 24.99% interest rates?

Christians who have gone through unemployment, costly medical procedures, and even divorce have on many occasion desired to pay back creditors, but instead those creditors respond to their requests for affordable payments with higher interest rates and elevated minimum payments. When this happens, the only remaining options may be a debt consolidation program or bankruptcy.

Conversely, some Christians have used bankruptcy as a way of avoiding payment of their debts, even when some changes to their lifestyle would allow them to pay the debts back. A single lady came to LifeChange Concepts back in 2006 with $58,000 in credit card debt. She had a well-paying job, making $46,000 annually, which would have allowed her to pay the debt off in about five years. In order to achieve this, she was going to have to give up a few things in her life and cut back on eating out. After two session, it became apparent that she was going to choose the easy way out. Before leaving that session, I cautioned her to do the hard work of understanding how she ended up with $58,000 (e.g. wrong attitudes about money), because if she didn't she would repeat the money management patterns that had gotten her to this point.

In truth, few people have debt because of financial setbacks. The problem goes back to ignorance, deceptions, or wrong attitudes about money (see Chapter Seven) which have allowed them to mismanage God's money over a period of time. The job loss or housing market crash is only the straw that broke the camel's back. My wife and I and many other Christians have gone through similar financial setbacks without running up a lot of debt and filing bankruptcy. The fact that many bankruptcy filers are repeat filers only confirms this. So, if you have filed bankruptcy or are considering it, I would ask you and your spouse to go deeper and determine why you are having financial problems.

> *Bankruptcy is not anymore dishonoring to God than the accumulation of the debt that required it.*
> —*Steve Smith, Certified Credit Counselor*
> *Plant City, FL*

Good Debt, Bad Debt

Before we look at the different types of debt to determine which have the Bible's seal of approval, let's remember that God's perfect plan is for each of us to owe nothing to anyone. Let me also remind you that, even in our debt-ridden economy, there are individuals and families of all ages that are debt-free. It's so exciting to see young couples that have put off buying a home and lived inexpensively for a period of time so that they could pay for their home in cash.

I recently met with a couple that had $118,300 of debt, which included their home mortgage, student loan, car loan, and credit card debt. Applying $1,600 per month to their debt until it was paid off would have resulted in them being debt-free in eight years. This approach, called the "snowball effect" or "compounding payment method," allows people to get debt-free over a very short period of time.

Now let's look at the different kinds of debt and see whether we can defend them as being good debt based on what we have learned about God's warning signs.

Credit Card Debt. Credit card debt does not have a biblical leg to stand on. It violates God's promises to provide for us and is idolatry (see Exodus 20:3–6 and Colossians 3:5).

> *Many people have finally realized that money can't buy happiness. Now they are using credit cards!*
>
> *—Anonymous*

Vehicle Loans. Vehicle loans violate the Bible warnings about interest, presumption of the future, and produces bondage. However, if you save up some money for a nice down payment and only borrow for twenty-four to thirty-six months, making your vehicle more valuable than the loan balance for the duration (leaving you the option to sell the vehicle if a financial setback occurs), you are not presuming on God as much. Of course, if you then kept your vehicle for another ten to fifteen years (and continued to save your monthly payment), you would always be able to pay cash for all future vehicles, and thus be in God's perfect will.

Student Loans. The world tells us that borrowing for an investment, like starting a business or going to college, is a good thing to do. They lump student loans in this group because the assumption is that a college degree will allow you to make more money over your lifetime, enabling you to use the higher income to pay back the debt. Tell this to the millions of college graduates who have tens of thousands of dollars in student loan debt that will take them twenty-five to thirty years to pay off. Over the past eight years, I have seen an increasing number of counselees with student loan debt that will take them that long to pay back. Some may never pay it off. I honestly believe that the default rate for student loans will continue to rapidly increase to the point where the government has to offer a forgiveness program. Currently, federal and state laws do not allow student loan debt to be discharged through bankruptcy.

Student loans seriously violate the presumption of the future warning, as well as the bondage and interest warnings. In fact, many graduating seniors couldn't even find jobs in 2010. Such loans also allow for the formation of bad habits by students (since all that loan money doesn't go for tuition) and for the parents, who often overspend for years rather than saving for future college tuition. There are many options for getting you or your children a college degree without incurring debt, such as military service or attending a military academy, working for a couple of years after high school to save for college, attending a local community college, living at home and working part-time, applying for scholarships and grants, starting to work and using an education reimbursement benefit to go to evening college, and excelling academically in high school in order to receive state scholarships.

Home Mortgage. Like the other debts, mortgages violate all of the Bible's warnings. However, because homes are usually appreciating assets (though many of you who bought a house in the 2005–2008 period might find this hard to believe), there is room to justify a mortgage. You can overcome the presumption warning by putting a twenty percent down payment on the house at closing and paying your mortgage down faster by adding $100–$200 extra to your mortgage payment each month. You can minimize the interest paid warning by either getting a fifteen-year mortgage or paying extra each month on a thirty-year mortgage. If you have done either of the above, you should be able to sell the house in the event of an economic setback without having to do a short sale.

Because lenders will almost always approve you for a loan amount greater than what you can afford, you must be diligent in no falling into the trap of buying too much house. Understanding the difference between what you really need in a house and what you want, and then buying what you need, is vital to you being the financial steward God wants you to be. So keep your covetous and prideful attitudes in check.

Having an emergency savings of three to six months of spending needs will also minimize the presumption warning.

Finally, when you have done all of the above, you will be more than likely living in a house that allows you to have a well-balanced lifestyle with little or no concern about missing payments and losing the house, thus minimizing or even eliminating any sense of bondage.

Cultivating Oneness with Debt

Because many women have a heartfelt need for security, having debt in one's marriage is a major obstacle to cultivating oneness. Together, gather up all the statements for your debts and then complete Form 2, which can be downloaded for free at my ministry website, www.lifechangeconcepts.org. Be sure to include interest rates, remaining payments, and accurate balances. Just getting all of this information on one page is a major step towards getting it paid off. Do not fear seeing Form 2 completed. It may be disheartening for some people, but for most couples it has motivated them to develop a plan to eliminate their debt completely.

Establish an amount that you can afford and, more importantly, are both in agreement on. Then begin paying that same amount each month until your debt is paid off. A word of caution: avoid the temptation to pay more than the agreed upon amount until you have at least $3,000 in your emergency savings account. The goal is to break the cycle of running back to the credit card every time there's an emergency, so using all surplus money to pay extra towards debt will almost always result in the continued use of debt. Two steps forward and one or two steps back is very discouraging and is not a formula for long-term success.

> **Key Point: The lender is not your friend, and in the end he wins.**

Additional Resources
Financial Peace, by Dave Ramsey.

One of the greatest blessings of our marriage has been a shared belief in financial responsibility and fiscal obedience to the Lord. That's not to say that we are perfect in our budget, but the fact that we are of one mind in our commitment to Godly financial stewardship has created a security and a peace of mind that is invaluable.

When we started our marriage journey less than three years ago, we were more in the negative than we wanted to be, but we were both committed to getting on track. It's hard to believe what the Lord can accomplish in a short period of time when your hearts are knitted together in financial oneness. At the beginning of our marriage, we had $10,000 of credit card debt, $10,000 of wedding debt, $10,000 of car debt, and little to no savings. We are grateful to God to report that all of those debts are now paid off, and we are well on our way toward saving three to six months' worth of spending.

We were both blessed to have been in tight financial situations before we met, where we saw God work through our obedience and faith in Him. We have come to understand that in regard to our giving, the Lord does not need or even want our money; rather, He wants our heart. We look at our giving not only as a chance to receive the joy that comes from helping others or our church, but as an opportunity to put our trust in Him.

We have learned (and are still learning) that discretion and discipline in our spending and budgeting is a rewarding endeavor. In regard to our long-term financial picture, we do not know what the future holds, but we know Who holds our future.

—Chris and Lora Weihe
Tampa, FL

Ray Lynch

CHAPTER FIFTEEN:
CREATING A VISION

Delight yourself in the Lord; and He will give you the desires of your heart. Commit your way to the Lord, trust also in Him, and He will do it.

Psalm 37:4-5

Big Rocks

While conducting a seminar on time management, a speaker once brought out a large glass jar completely filled with big rocks. He asked the group if the jar was full. Everyone responded, "Yes." He then proceeded to empty a container of small pebbles into the jar with the rocks until the pebbles reached the top. He asked again if the jar was full. The group had caught on and responded, "No." He told them they were correct, and proceeded to pour sand into the jar until it, again appeared full. The group correctly maintained that the jar was still not full. Finally, the speaker poured water into the jar with the rocks, pebbles, and sand, until it truly was full. At last, he asked the group to state the purpose of his demonstration. After a number of incorrect guesses, the speaker revealed his point: if you don't put the big rocks in first, you won't be able to get them in at all.

The "big rocks" in our lives are the things that are important to us, our priorities. Big rocks are our goals, and maybe even a dream or two. What are your financial goals? If you are the average couple, you don't have any written financial goals. You may have some goals, but they're just floating around in your head. If this is the case with you, "floating around in your head" isn't a good place for your goals to be—for two reasons. First, most head goals are never achieved, while most written goals are. Second, head goals result in arguments and confusion in a marriage because one spouse doesn't know what is important to the other.

Written Financial Goals

Surveys consistently show that people who write down their goals are more likely to achieve them than the people who don't. Written goals are more real and concrete than unwritten goals, which leads the person who has written them out to create a plan to achieve them.

The further away the completion of the goal is (say, a long-term goal of twenty years), the less likely it is to be achieved if not written down. For example, most parents say they want to pay for their child's college, but few ultimately do. The child is born and then the weeks turn into months and the months turn into years and before they know it the child is graduating from high school and they have no money saved.

My parents paid for my sister's and my college tuition and room and board, leaving us with the responsibility for books and personal expenses. Thus, we graduated without debt. What a legacy! My father was the sole provider and his income was moderate for that time period. My mom was a stay-at-home mom. So, how did they do it? Did they receive an inheritance? No. Did they contribute to a prepaid college fund? No. Did my dad receive a big bonus every year? No. Did my sister and I receive scholarships? No. My father was the first in our family to get a college degree and he and my mom believed it was important for me and my sister to get college degrees (which we did). It was a "big rock" to them, so they developed a plan to achieve it. The plan included few vacations growing up, one car for the family (which my sister and I shared with our parents when we got our driver's licenses), and eating out as a family just once per year. I remember this clearly, because it would happen on Easter Sunday, when we'd go the Avenue Restaurant in Rehoboth Beach, Delaware. In addition, they lived on a written budget (after all, my dad was an accountant) and my mother used cash envelopes for most expense categories. My sister and I did not have the latest electronic equipment in our rooms. Of course, we didn't spend very much time inside anyway. We had one TV and one phone for the house, but we never felt deprived.

Today, most parents think it is more important to give their children every new gadget that comes along, buy them their own cars when they turn sixteen, allow them to experience every type of activity there is in the world, and give them a Disney World vacation every year. Then they send them off to college and help them get the student loans to boot. If you are a young couple with young children or your first child planned for the future, I hope you will pay attention to this chapter, as well as the rest of the book.

You can go through life reacting to the events and people in your life, or you can be proactive. By identifying your big rocks and creating a budget that allows you to achieve many of them, you will be dictating how you will give, save, and spend, rather than being subject to the desires of family members and friends. You won't be like the one family I counseled that let their first-grader go to twenty-five of his classmate's birthday parties, because that was what the school and the majority of parents were doing. Instead, you will have a budget for gift money for your child's real friends' birthday parties—maybe two or three of them. When your wealthy friends want you to join them for a costly vacation, you can confidently say no. When church members are constantly inviting you to join them for a restaurant meal after church, you can tell them that your God-honoring budget and financial goals only allow you to do that once per month. When your child is pestering you for the latest cell phone, you can remind them that you will be paying for much of their college expenses.

The more clearly defined a goal, the more likely it is to be attained. Your financial goals should be *measurable*. They should also be *reasonable*. My parents' goal was to provide enough for each of us to attend a moderately priced college. I went to the state school, which allowed them to pay all the tuition and room and board. It would not have been reasonable for me to attend an expensive private school. My parents had also determined what they could afford to save and how much that would result in by the time we were ready for college. Because they had a target, they could measure how they were doing each year. If they were behind, they would save a little bit more going forward.

What Would You Do?

As I have done in a couple of previous chapters, I've created a financial goals scenario for you and your spouse to work through. In this chapter, the scenario deals with establishing financial goals. This will give you a little practice time before tackling your financial goals, and maybe even give you some things to think about that you had not considered.

You and your husband have decided that you will stop working in order to be a stay-at-home mom when your first child is born (hopefully within the next three years). Currently, both of you work full-time and your husband's salary is slightly higher than yours. Your very best friends are encouraging you to move into their apartment complex when your lease is up in sixty days. The rent would be $250 more than you currently pay, and the move would add ten minutes to both your husband's and your commute to work. Until now, you've been saving $375 per month. You have two debts: a car loan for which you pay $295 per month (and which will be paid off in eleven months) and a student loan, due to be paid off in eight years at the current payment of $144 per month. Your savings account balance is $3,900. You have no credit card debt.

1. What are your choices for where to live for the coming year?

2. What is your number one financial goal?

3. What other financial goals might you have?

4. If you move into your friend's complex, what budget expense categories would be impacted?

5. Which choice creates the best opportunity to achieve your goals?

Did your goals include investing in your husband's career (taking into account, for example, additional schooling) in order to increase his income, buying a house before the child comes along, or paying off all of your debt? Did you know that by applying the

$295 car payment to the student loan (adding it to the current $144 per month payment for a total payment of $439) after the car is paid off in eleven months, you would be able to pay off the student loan in three years and three months? Would this information change your goals?

Key Point: If you don't identify your big rocks and put them in the jar of life first, you won't be able to get them in at all.

Cultivating Oneness when Setting Financial Goals

1. Pray for God's goals to become clear to you.

2. Both of you make a list of financial goals you would like to achieve and the time period you would like to complete them.

3. Discuss each goal with your spouse (for example, why is this goal important to you, and what are your thoughts on how to achieve it?) and allow your spouse to ask questions and offer thoughts after you are done explaining each goal. For now, focus on your big rocks.

4. Did you include any of your dreams from Chapter Five as written financial goals?

CHAPTER SIXTEEN:
BUDGETING 101

Commit your works to the Lord and your plans will be established.

Proverbs 16:3

Budgeting vs. Record Keeping

Some of the couples who have come to me for counseling over the years have kept good records of what they've spent, but they have never budgeted. A recent counselee at LifeChange Concepts thought record keeping and budgeting were one and the same thing. Obviously they were quite surprised when I told them that they were not. Good record keeping is an important part of budgeting, but it is not budgeting. Budgeting is planning (*looking forward*) what you will spend by expense category against what you will earn over a period of time, typically one year, while record keeping is *looking back* at what you have done.

A previous LCC client had this to say about budgeting: "I'm constantly hearing from other couples that they have a budget, but they really don't. What they mean is that they don't have money in the bank right now to go out to dinner, or buy that outfit, etc. or... the wife is okay with that purchase, but the husband is not... or vice versa. That's not what a *budget* is! I'm often taken aback by some purchases that others make, wondering how that was even possible. My husband reminds me that these families simply don't have a budget, but instead probably put much of their spending on a credit card."

Money Is a Finite Resource

Your budget should attempt to achieve as many of your "big rocks" as possible. If your budget achieves little rocks at the expense of your big rocks, then either your big rocks really were not big rocks, or you need to redo your budget so that it will achieve your big rocks. For instance, if saving for your daughter's college fund is a big rock and taking a nice family vacation each year is a little rock, and you have $150 per month set aside in your proposed budget for vacation and zero dollars for the college fund, then either vacations are more important than a college fund or you need to create a budget that accounts for more savings for the college fund and less for vacations. You may even decide that another currently-funded expense category is less important than both the college fund and vacation and therefore can be cut.

Few people in the world have enough income to do all the things they want to do in life. Money is a finite resource that requires each of us to decide what things are the most important to us. Unfortunately, as I discussed in Chapter Fourteen, credit card availability has allowed people to think that there really is a money tree and that they can have it all. We should thank God daily for the fact that He does not give us enough to satisfy all our desires. If He did so, I believe life would become very boring and we would be in great danger of living a self-dependent life rather than a God-dependent life.

King Solomon, the richest man of his day, wrote the Book of Ecclesiastes at the end of his life. This is what he said about having enough to do everything he wanted to do:

> *All that my eyes desired I did not refuse them. I did not withhold my heart from any pleasure, for my heart was pleased because of all my labor and this was my reward for all my labor. Thus I considered all my activities which my hands had done and the labor which I had exerted, and behold all was vanity and striving after wind and there was no profit under the sun.*
>
> *Ecclesiastes 2:10–11, emphasis added*

Solomon looked back on his life and realized that he had done a lot that brought no glory to God. I bet he wished someone had taught him how to budget when he was a young man! A Christian should have a plan for how he will give, save, and spend God's money, and this plan should be consistent with God's Word (see Chapters Nine through Fourteen) and His will for your life.

I Can't Budget Because…

Over the years, I have heard many reasons why people don't budget: they were never taught, their income varies month to month, they don't make enough money, it's too confining, and they always have a surplus so they don't need it. The truth is, everyone needs to budget. Even King Solomon needed a budget. We have all heard the saying, "To fail to plan is a plan to fail." As you work through the budgeting process, you will allow God to work on your hearts and you will create oneness in your marriage. So let's begin the process.

Budgeting 101

Step One: Determine where your money is currently going and how much income you have coming in each month. From my website, complete Forms 1–3 (in Form 3, complete only the "past" column at this time). It is helpful to be as accurate as you can, so take the time to review the past two to four months of bank statements and credit card statements to see where you have been spending God's money. Divide up the work of reviewing these statements so that each of you feels involved. If one of you is more number savvy than the other, take time to explain the process to the less savvy spouse as you go along. Be patient and kind.

Step Two: Pray and seek God's wisdom through His Word and godly counsel in order to know His will for how you should give, save, and spend His money over the next twelve months. Also ask Him to give you a humble, self-sacrificing, trusting, and contented heart. Pray that He will bring unity through this process. Psalm 119:2 says, *"How blessed are those who observe His testimonies, who seek Him with all their heart."* As you study and meditate on the scriptures in this book and the Bible, God will reveal His will for your finances, and from that you will develop your giving, saving, and spending plan for the coming year.

In addition to reading and studying the Bible, seek godly counsel. *"Without consultation, plans are frustrated, but with many counselors they succeed"* (Proverbs 15:22). I failed to follow this strategy in my early years as a Christian. Pride and fear kept me from sharing my plans with other Christians. In my years of counseling, I see the same pride and fear keeping others from getting counsel. In particular, starting new businesses can be a damaging area in your family's finances. Without counsel, plans and businesses fail, so be sure to seek out godly counsel before starting a business.

Proverbs 19:21 says, *"Many plans are in a man's heart, but the counsel of the Lord will stand."* When selecting people for counsel, be sure to look for men and women who are studying the Bible and living for the Lord. Psalm 1:1 tells us that we will be blessed if we *"[walk] not in the counsel of the ungodly."* Which people in your life are giving you financial counsel? Do they meet the standard set by Proverbs 12:21 and Psalm 1:1? If they often say "in my opinion" rather than "the Bible says," your advisors may be doing more harm than good.

Step Three: Examine each expense category (including giving and saving) and determine which ones do not line up with God's Word and your goals. This part of the process is important, because the manner in which you currently divide up God's money between giving, saving, and spending is probably not what He wants. For instance, you may be giving ten percent and saving ten percent and still aren't in God's will. There may be parts of your "spending" that have become idols and therefore must be let go.

Review Chapters Ten through Fourteen as you complete this phase of the budgeting process. Remember that this is a joint effort. Both of you need to be involved in this step.

Step Four: Begin to modify your current spending (i.e. the "past" column) in order to create the giving, saving, and spending that God wants for your family. My website offers many ways to reduce spending in each of the categories shown on Form 3. Modifying budget amounts requires you to make real changes. You can't just say that you'll reduce "Electric/Gas" from $140 to $125 without changing the thermostat setting or closing the blinds. You and your spouse will need to discuss the details of how to accomplish each change. If an action is required to complete the change (e.g.

eliminating options or reducing minutes on your cell phone), then assign the task to one of you and set a date for it to be completed.

The process of creating a God-honoring, balanced budget can be simplified by first eliminating all expense categories that are under contract or cannot be reasonably changed at this time and focusing on the remaining expense categories. Of the remaining categories, start with those where you can make painless reductions (such as reducing your auto insurance premium by getting three or more quotes), then move on to the discretionary expense categories (like food, eating out, clothing, gifts, haircuts, etc.) to find the additional reductions necessary to bring your budget into compliance with God's will. Avoid the temptation to shortchange categories such as house repairs, vehicle repairs and medical expenses so you can have more money for eating out or vacations.

Every expense category in your budget is made up of *quantity* or *quality* choices that you'll have to make. As you create your spending boundaries, examine each category from this quantity/quality perspective. Doing so will allow you to find ways to reduce your spending without totally giving up that category.

Let's look at a couple of expense categories to see how this works. Eating out has many quality/quantity choices. Quality choices include eating at an expensive restaurant rather than an inexpensive one, choosing the filet mignon instead of spaghetti, having dessert, or buying the latte coffee instead of plain coffee. Quantity choices include how many times you'll go out to eat or whether to split an entree or not. You may prefer to eat well when you go out, in which you'll have to reduce the number (quantity) of times you eat out in order to reduce your spending in this category. Another couple that just enjoys going out may switch to less expensive places to continue eating out the same number of times. My wife and I fall into this latter group. We enjoy just having breakfast together at Chick-fil-A once a week as opposed to one dinner at nice restaurant.

Cable TV offers quantity/quality choices. You can have cable on four TVs or one (quantity) or you can get the deluxe or the basic package (quality). You may watch two pay-for-view movies per month or none (quantity and quality). The choice is yours. But choose carefully, remembering that you are limited to the income God provides you (no consumer debt) and knowing that giving and saving are important components of a biblical steward's budget.

Income Deficit

During my twenty-two years of counseling, I have found that about one in twenty-five counselees are unable to balance income and spending no matter how much they cut spending, because they do not have enough income to cover their basic needs. I believe the Bible says other family members and the church should help these families after their savings have been depleted.

Aside from those who are temporarily unemployed or underemployed, however, there are some people who, through their own laziness or their inability to rely on God's strength to overcome minor disabilities, refuse to become the productive people God desires. I have seen husbands who would play video games rather than work, people who keep getting college degrees (and living off their student loans) rather than work, adult children living off their parents rather than work, and people with minor disabilities trying to live off a $950 disability check per month rather than work. Whenever the latter come in for counseling, I think of my friend Bill Renje, who is paralyzed from the waist down and yet works and supports his stay-at-home wife and three children. I also think of my friend Steve, who almost died and was in the hospital for months, who refused a wheelchair and handicap sticker for his car when offered by the doctor during his discharge from the hospital. Although he only had the strength to walk across the room with a walker at the time, he told the doctor that he was a child of God and that God had not made him to be in the wheelchair. Steve also wisely understood that if he used the wheelchair instead of the walker, he would never get better.

Steve and Bill are overcomers in Christ. Too many Christians today deny the power of God in their lives by giving in to their disability and thus resigning themselves to a life of continuous financial struggles. Many of these issues may require a licensed Christian counselor to help you work through, so don't be afraid to get help.

Step Five: Commit your plan (budget) and life to God, trust His promises, and obey His principles on money. Proverbs 16:3 says, *"Commit your works to the Lord and your plans will be established."* Remembering those foundational truths discussed in Chapter Six, it is now time to commit your plan into God's Hands. Commit means to give in trust. You will not trust the credit cards when things don't go as planned. Instead you commit to go to God in prayer and to wait and trust Him in those circumstances. You commit not to disrespect your spouse by willfully violating the budget. You commit to discuss and resolve financial issues with your spouse when "life" happens. God said, *"I will never desert you, nor will I ever forsake you"* (Hebrews 11:5), so put your focus on obedience and leave the circumstances of life to God.

After starting your budget, there will be times when you find God's direction to be completely out of step with what seems logical and what everyone else is doing (even many in the church). In those situations, be illogical and follow God's direction regardless. Trust and obey, for there is no other way.

In Chapter Eighteen, I will discuss your monthly budget meetings and making adjustments as circumstances trump your budget so that you can successfully navigate life and grow in the Lord.

> **Key Point: A budget provides a forum to share your priorities and goals and fosters communication in your marriage, which builds trust and intimacy.**

Cultivate Oneness during the Budget-Creating Process

1. Both spouses must be involved in this process.

2. Be open and honest, but be kind.

3. Bathe the entire process in prayer.

4. Stay focused on your "big rocks."

5. Remember that your spouse brings value to this process.

6. Become selfless.

Additional Resources

A Chosen Bullet: A Broken Man's Triumph through Faith and Sports, by Bill Renje.

Ray Lynch

CHAPTER SEVENTEEN:
VICTORIOUS LIVING, PART 1 –
CASH ENVELOPES

*All that my eyes desired I did not refuse them. I did not
withhold my heart from any pleasure…*

Ecclesiastes 2:10

The budget you have developed isn't worth the paper it's written
on unless you have an effective budget control system in place. We
are human. Even though we are covered by the blood of Jesus and
have the mind of Christ, we have the potential to wander back into
our old habits and attitudes.

A budget control system has two components to help you
victoriously live out your budget: cash envelopes, which will be
discussed in this chapter, and monthly budget review meetings,
which will be discussed in Chapter Eighteen. The system outlined
in these chapters is simple and requires minimal bookkeeping,
which is important for those of us who are trying to simplify our
lives so we can spend more time with the Lord and with family.

The Purpose of Cash Envelopes

It controls discretionary spending. Many studies have found that people who use credit cards spend on average twenty-five to thirty percent more than people who use cash. In addition, people who use debit cards also spend more than people who use cash. Using credit cards and debit cards separates the pleasure of buying from the pain of paying, and therefore results in higher spending. One of my class attendees put it more succinctly when he said, "When you pay by credit card or debit card, they give you the card back. But when you pay by cash, they keep it!" Recent studies have found that people who use credit cards to purchase things experience the same stimulus in their brains as cocaine addicts do when they are using cocaine. It's easy to see why companies want us to use credit and debit cards when shopping.

Using cash for discretionary expense categories (food, clothing, eating out, gifts, etc.) will help you to stay within your budgeted amounts. The cash envelopes offer a finite and visible boundary (your budgeted amount) that, if respected, will result in you becoming a better planner and more frequently using the word "no" in your daily life. In the end, you will join the ten percent of Americans who achieve their "big rocks." If it's any comfort to you, I have never heard of anyone who uses the cash envelope for food and starved.

It simplifies bookkeeping. When you start using cash instead of your debit card for the discretionary expense categories, the number of entries into your checkbook register (this is for the ten of you who actually keep a checkbook register when using a debit card) and on your bank statement will be significantly reduced, so that you could actually maintain your checkbook register and reconcile it to your monthly bank statement in a matter of minutes.

Technology, like debit cards and online banking, have made it more difficult to keep up with your finances, not easier. It amazes me how many people tell me they don't have time to keep a checkbook register, and yet they spend numerous times each day checking their balances online, presumably so they won't overdraft their account. The good news is that using cash envelopes will greatly simplify your life and your finances, allowing you to maintain your checkbook register and have the peace of mind of knowing you won't spend money you don't have.

Purchasing items with cash eliminates the need to keep receipts, except for items that may be returned, such as clothing.

System Requirements

If you agree to use cash envelopes to help keep your spending in line with your budget(and I pray that you will), you need to agree to the following terms:

- All expenditures are paid for by check, cash, or credit card (I'll discuss the credit card use a bit later in this chapter) and all check transactions will be recorded in your checkbook register.

- You will have only one personal checking account. A second account would be required if you have a business.

- All income, except personal gifts, should be deposited in the personal checking account. Unexpected or one-time income such as yard sale proceeds, bonuses, tax refunds, and rebates should also be deposited in the checking account. For people not on a budget, these types of income are often spent on whatever their current desires are. When you are on a budget, you stay within the spending boundaries you have established and agreed to, and the extra income goes in the checking account. The reason for not spending this money is that you don't know whether or not this was God's provision for an upcoming expense, like a major car or house repair that's not in your budget. If you already have your six months of emergency savings and no credit card debt, the family certainly has the option to use some or all of these funds for something discretionary. If you have debt and little savings, you would be wise to stick to your budget and put this money in the bank.

Setting Up the Envelope System

Determine which budget categories will be cash only. I've had couples have anywhere from six to twenty-seven envelopes, with the average being around eight or nine. Since the primary purpose of the envelopes is to control spending, you must decide how much control you need. The couple with twenty-seven envelopes obviously felt like they needed a lot of control. The most frequently chosen budget categories for cash envelopes include household items, food, eating out, clothing, work lunches, haircuts, dry cleaning, gifts, allowances, and marriage enrichment.

Use adult allowances. If you do not have children, I recommend adult allowances where each spouse receives the portion of some of the budget categories (like haircuts, clothing, personal items, and work lunches) that was going to be used by them. If you have adult allowances, for those selected categories there will not be a family envelope. The allowance allows each spouse to make personal spending decisions without consulting their mate. This approach will actually enhance oneness in your marriage, because it eliminates petty bickering over who is using up the family envelope. In addition to the adult allowances, you can have family envelopes for categories like eating out, dry cleaning, food, and household items. Family envelopes cultivate oneness when each of you demonstrates wisdom and godly attitudes in using these monies.

Calculate the envelope amounts. If you're just starting out on cash envelopes, I recommend filling the envelopes on *one* of your paydays (if both spouses are working). This will give you shorter periods between fill-ups and make it less likely you will run out of money. If the payday is twice per month, divide your monthly budget amount by two to calculate the envelope amounts. If it is biweekly, divide the budget amount by 2.17 (twenty-six paychecks per year divided by twelve months per year). If weekly, divide by 4.33 (fifty-two paychecks per year divided by twelve months per year). Write the budget category and the amount per fill-up on your envelopes.

Fill your envelopes. On payday (again, you only fill your envelopes on one spouse's payday, if both work), one of you must go to the bank with a check made out to "Cash" for the total you will need. *Do not use the ATM*, since you will not be able to get the small-denomination bills you may need. It would be very helpful to the bank teller to attach a post-it to the check showing the breakdown of each denomination (for example, 5 - $50s = $250).

Often Asked Questions

Can we use our debit or credit cards? Some expenditures require a credit or debit card (like purchasing airline tickets) and others that are more convenient if a credit or debit card is used (like buying gasoline). Therefore, we do not rule out the use of either. However, you are encouraged to limit the use of the card. Remember, the use of cash will eliminate most of the expenditures where you previously used the card. A credit card is preferred over a debit card because it requires only one checkbook register entry each month and you are protected in the event it is stolen and used (lending laws limit your liability to a maximum of $50.00 if you report you card stolen within forty-eight hours). You do not have the same protection with your debit card.

You still must save your receipts in order to confirm the accuracy of your credit card statement, and all credit card purchases should be within your budgeted boundaries. You must pay off the total balance each month. You should agree to cut up the card the first month you can't pay off the total credit card balance.

What happens when the envelope runs dry? You stop spending until your next cash fill-up. You won't do this too many times before you begin to adapt your spending decisions to your budget. For the first three months on your budget, you're still trying to figure out what should go in each category. Therefore, as long as you have surplus built into your budget, you could use your debit card to purchase food if you run out of food money before the next fill-up. Then, when you total your expenditures for food that month (using Form 9, which will be discussed in Chapter Eighteen), it will include the cash envelope total as well as the debit charge. After three months you may have to adjust your budget for food higher and then stop using the debit card completely. Again, you can only do this if you have surplus in your budget or if you can reduce another expense category by the amount you are raising your food expenses.

Who pays the bills? One person should pay the bills. Select the person who enjoys doing it. There is usually one in each family. You should have only one personal joint checking account (unless you have a business, in which case you should have a separate business account) and all personal transactions should be handled with this account.

Do we need to keep receipts? The only receipts you need to keep are for those items paid by your credit card, or an item bought by cash that may need to be returned (such as clothing). The receipts from cash purchases can be kept in the envelope.

Where should we keep the money? One of the disciplines of a biblical steward is to plan your spending and avoid impulsive shopping. Therefore, some money will be carried in your purse or wallet, but most of your money will remain in the envelopes at home until you are ready to use it. Keep your envelopes in a hidden place, like your dresser drawer, and don't tell the neighbors that you're keeping $500 in cash in your house.

What do we do if there's money still in the envelope at the time of the next fill-up? First of all, some envelope categories (such as clothing, haircuts, and household items) will have money left in the envelope, because these funds are not spent every month. For these categories, allow the money to accumulate until it is needed. However, other categories (such as food and eating out) may also have money left in the envelope at the end of the pay period, particularly if you are starting cash envelopes and a budget for the first time. In this situation, your budget amount may not accurately match your true need for this category and it could take three to six months before you determine the actual amount needed. In the event that you have overstated the amount needed in your budget, you may experience having leftover money in the envelope at the end of the pay period. If this happens, fold the money in half, paperclip it, and put it back in the envelope. If this surplus continues to occur for three months, you should consider lowering your budget amount by the average monthly amount of the surplus. The three-month surplus can then be given, saved, spent, or used to pay down debt as you two agree.

> **Key Point: Using cash envelopes will simplify your finances and bring peace to the family.**

Cultivating Oneness through a Cash Lifestyle

Earlier in the book, I discussed most women's heartfelt need for security. One thing that helps a woman to feel secure is knowing that all the bills can be paid on time and that she won't receive a notice from the bank that the checking account has been overdrawn in order to do so. Using cash instead of credit and debit cards and keeping your checkbook register current (which is much easier to do when using cash) so you don't write checks when there's insufficient funds in your account, will bring great peace to your wife's heart. Over the years, testimony after testimony from wives verifies this.

If you commit to living within your budget boundaries, and you use cash envelopes to make those boundaries firm, you will adapt your spending patterns (a life change) to fit your budget. Within three to six months, your adjustment will be such that you'll be comfortable in your new lifestyle. This won't happen if you believe that your budget amounts are "general guidelines" for your life and you continually justify overspending.

So, start using cash envelopes as soon as you have developed your budget and enjoy the peace that will come over your marriage.

The counseling at LifeChange Concepts showed us that there are two ways to live financially: God's way and the world's way. We had many wrong attitudes about money that we had to address before creating our first spending plan. Using the cash envelopes now helps us to control our spending and stay on budget. I used to write endless checks, but now I enjoy the ease and simplicity of paying for many things like groceries and clothing using cash. When the envelope is empty, I know it's time to stop spending.

Of course, it didn't take long before our spending got into step with our cash envelopes. I used to think that a budget would be constraining, but now I feel free just knowing that by following our spending plan we can make it through the month.

Finally, we are also learning to trust in our Father to provide for us and to wait on His timing, rather than rush ahead of Him and make a costly mistake.

—Dave and Kelly Partin
Tampa, FL

CHAPTER EIGHTEEN:
VICTORIOUS LIVING, PART II—
MONTHLY BUDGET REVIEW
MEETINGS

For which one of you, when he wants to build a tower, does not first sit down and calculate the cost to see if he has enough to complete it?

Luke 14:28

The Purpose

Monthly budget review meetings are a critical part of cultivating oneness in your marriage through finances. These meetings are the time when you account for your spending (by expense category) and income (God's provision) for the previous month. Each meeting should start with prayer, thanking God for His provision and for giving you wisdom to manage His money. You may have to ask for forgiveness if you have used some of His money in a way that was outside of His will.

These meetings are important because *they keep both spouses current on the family finances.* The spouse who isn't paying the bills will know how the family is doing, and therefore can provide intelligent and informed counsel when future financial issues come up for discussion. Remember, your spouse is your number one counselor after God, and as a result your family will make better decisions when both spouses are fully aware of the family finances.

> *The way of a fool is right in his own eyes, but a wise man is he who listens to counsel.*
>
> Proverbs 12:15

Having both spouses current on the family finances is also helpful in the event of the death of the spouse who has been doing the bill paying and other bookkeeping responsibilities. Too often I have counseled surviving spouses who did not know anything about the family finances. They couldn't even tell me what bills needed to be paid. As a result, their grief is magnified by frustrations brought on by not knowing what to do. Some surviving spouses actually feel anger towards their deceased mate, which creates an unhealthy grieving process.

In addition to the monthly meetings, the bill-paying spouse should allow their mate to pay the bills from time to time. Be gentle with them and explain the process without getting mad. Finally, it would be a good idea to leave written instructions for your spouse explaining who to call (with phone numbers) regarding life insurance policies, investments, and other financial issues.

Having both spouses engaged in the finances through these meetings also makes it less likely that one spouse will hide spending from the other (See Chapter Four).

Finally, these meetings are important because *they allow you to more quickly see the need to revise your budget*. No matter how well thought out a budget is, the year very likely won't go as planned. This is because *life* happens. More car repairs are required than planned, emergency root canals and crowns cause you to exceed your medical budget, and emergency trips to visit ailing parents aren't foreseen. What do most families do when these things occur? They put these expenses on the credit card! They do this because they don't keep track of their income and expenses. Denying that there's a problem will not make the problem go away.

> *The fear of the Lord is the beginning of knowledge; fools despise wisdom and instruction.*
>
> *Proverbs 1:7*

By tracking your monthly income and expenses, you will be able to identify overspending or falling income more quickly and make the necessary budget revisions. Knowledge is all that separates a family that's in debt and failing to achieve their goals from a family that's staying out of debt and achieving their goals. Although there is a small percentage of people who will fail even if given this information, I have learned that most people, when seeing danger, will make good decisions. So, the key is seeing the danger.

> *The prudent sees the evil and hides himself, but the naïve go on, and are punished for it.*
>
> *Proverbs 22:3*

Tracking Your Income and Expenses

My wife and I have been tracking our income and expenses monthly since 1989. We use Form 9, which can be downloaded for free from www.lifechangeconcepts.org. However, if you have the ability to do it on the computer, have at it. The only disadvantage of doing it on the computer is that both spouses aren't participating in the creation of the report.

If you decide to use Form 9 and do the report manually, here are the steps:

1. Bring your calculator, highlighter, pencil, checkbook register, and credit card statement to the meeting. Each transaction in your checkbook should note the date of the transaction, the check number, who the check was for, the amount of the check and, most importantly, which expense category the expenditure was charged to. Before the meeting, whoever pays the bills should summarize the transactions on the credit card statement by expense category. This will make the completion of Form 9 much easier.

2. One person is responsible for completing Form 9. They have the calculator and pencil. You use a pencil, because your spouse may miss an expenditure recorded in the checkbook register for one or more expense categories the first time you ask for them, requiring you to go back and change a category amount. Trust me when I tell you that we all do it, so don't think your spouse is just trying to irritate you.

3. The other person has the checkbook register, credit card statement, and the highlighter. The reason for this is that it's better to use the checkbook register than the bank statement; the bank statement may not include a check that was written during the month you are recording, because the receiver of that check may not cash it in the same month it was issued.

4. The person with Form 9 starts with the first budget category and asks for all expenditures for that category. The person with the checkbook register and credit card statement reads off all expenditures, highlighting them as they go (so that you know that you've given them to your spouse). Go through each category until all expenses are accounted for on Form 9. *Remember, Form 9 is a picture of what has happen to your checking account for the month—cash in, cash out.* This is the reason that you record all the money that went into the cash envelopes as being spent, even if there's still money in the envelope at the end of the month. All of the cash put into your envelopes was removed from your checking account when you wrote the cash check, and thus is considered spent. When giving the expenditures to the person who is recording on Form 9, round off the amounts to the closest whole number. Keep it simple, so you won't mind doing it for the rest of your life!

5. Total the deposits for the month and record them at the bottom of Form 9. Note that you are only totaling new income. Money transferred from your savings account is not new money.

6. Total your expenses and subtract them from your income to determine whether you exceeded your budget or had a surplus.

Analyzing Form 9

You want to analyze Form 9 each month in order to see how you are doing. Here are some things you want to look at:

- The bottom line—did you have a surplus or deficit?

- Compare the total expenses to your total budgeted amount—are you under budget?

- Examine each budget category to see how you did versus your budget, and how the amounts impacted the bottom line. For example, if your total expenses were exactly equal to your total budget and you had zero expenses for medical, car repairs, and auto insurance (because you pay it every six months), could there be a problem? Maybe, if these undercharges were not offset by an overcharge in another category, such as spending most of your vacation money in that month. If that is not the case, you are probably overspending in your discretionary categories and are headed for trouble.

- Examine your cash categories. Were you on budget? You should be. If you're not, why? Talk about it. If you're filling your envelopes on a biweekly basis, for ten of the months those categories should be below budget, since you only received two paychecks and your budget amount is for 2.17 paychecks (see Chapter Seveteen). For the two months when you receive three paychecks, the envelope categories will be greater than your budget amounts. (If you stay within your envelope amounts, the total of the twelve months divided by twelve will equal your monthly budgeted amount.) However, since your income will be higher because of the third paycheck, you should still have a surplus for the month, even though your envelope categories are higher.

- Are the categories that fluctuate monthly (such car and house repairs) running ahead of the annual budget amount earlier than they should be? If you had budgeted $1200 for the year for car repairs ($100 per month) and by the end of June (mid-year) you had spent $1100, what should you do? Wouldn't it be prudent to raise the budget to $150 per month (which adds another $600 for the year)? If you do this, won't you need to reduce spending somewhere else?

Key Point: Tracking your income and expenses together on a monthly basis is second in importance only to praying together as the way to cultivate oneness in your marriage through finances.

Cultivating Oneness through Monthly Budget Review Meetings

When we were first married, my wife did not enjoy sitting down together each month to review our spending and income. It was something totally foreign to her and she didn't see the need for it. Anyway, I did the bookkeeping and she trusted me to do a good job. Although I appreciated her confidence in me, I knew she needed to be involved for all the reasons outlined in this book.

So, I made her do it! And to her credit, she did sit down with me. By the way, today she is the one asking when we are going to do Form 9. One of you may need to encourage your spouse do it also. The Bible says that the husband is the spiritual leader of his family. This does not mean he pays all the bills, handles all the finances, and makes all the financial decisions. What it does mean, however, is that he is to *lead*. Part of leading is scheduling a monthly budget review meeting *every* month.

1. Have you completed or are nearing completion of your written budget?

2. Have you completed the budget category and budgeted amount columns on Form 9 so that you're ready to begin tracking your spending and income?

As a young married couple with two small children living on one income, money is very tight for us. As a result, we have come to realize that we need to stick to a budget. We have decided that one person should be in charge of writing the checks, balancing the checkbook, and overseeing the in/out flow of the money. We meet together once a month to go over the budget and see if there have been any changes.

Our monthly budget meetings are always scheduled for times after the kids have gone to bed so we can devote our complete attention to our finances. We try not to argue or point fingers if there have been any discrepancies. Instead, we remain focused on why the budget is so important.

In our budget, we set aside a small amount each week that is strictly "fun" money for each of us. How we choose to spend this money is up to both of us. This helps us feel that we can have a little fun with the money we do make. Also, we set aside another small amount for "our time," without the children. This money could be for a dinner out or getting coffee together. This "date" money is to be used only for what Kim and I can do together without the children. Our goal is to date twice a month.

While money may not bring happiness, we believe it can make things in a marriage easier. When there is not enough to go around, it can be a major catalyst for disagreements in a marriage. Therefore, we work hard to stay on-budget by working together so we can achieve our common goals. By doing so, we have discovered that a little bit can go a long way.

—Brian and Kim Ostry
Damascus, MD

SUMMARY

During the American Revolution, the army under the command of General George Washington lost and avoided more battles than they won. General Washington had the wisdom to know that winning a battle, though possible in some cases, would result in too many casualties. This would then leave his army too weak to fight future battles. A strategy of "win at all costs" would have lost the war. He understood that his small, ill-equipped army was no match for direct confrontation with the much larger and better equipped British army. Therefore, his normal strategy was to strike the enemy and then run, or avoid the British army altogether. And yet we all know that he and his army won the war. Applying a similar strategy in our marriages can help us to win the war. Winning the war, in this case, is having a great marriage.

George Washington was an incredibly humble man, and because of this he was not only willing to lose battles but also to withstand the scorn of the many people who didn't have his tactical wisdom or humility. In marriage, pride often drives us to win the battles. We win the financial arguments or strong-arm our spouse during the financial decision-making process so that the outcomes are to our liking. This was the case when I forced Judy into agreeing to lease the minivan (see Chapter Seven). But at what cost do we win these battles? Over time, a continual stream of these so called "victories" will weaken the marriage relationship and the war will be lost. The end result is divorce or, at best, two people still living together but emotionally separated.

Someone once said that humility is not thinking less of yourself, but thinking more of others. The Apostle Paul, in writing to the church of Ephesus, said this about cultivating oneness:

> *Therefore I, the prisoner of the Lord, implore you to walk in a manner worthy of the calling with which you have been called, with all humility and gentleness, with patience, showing tolerance for one another in love, being diligent to preserve the unity of the Spirit in the bond of peace.*
>
> *Ephesians 4:1–3*

Although Paul wasn't speaking about the marriage relationship, the principles he laid out, if followed in our relationship with our spouse, will result in a great marriage. How are you doing? Note that I didn't ask how your spouse was doing. I asked how *you* are doing with regards to living out Ephesians 4:1–3.

When looking to improve our marriage relationship and finances, we should look no further than ourselves. Each of us has the ability and power of God to change ourselves so that we conform to the image of God. So, examine yourself and leave to God the changes you think you want to make in your spouse. You may find that after God changes you, your spouse actually looks pretty good just the way they are.

Very early in our marriage, Judy and I discovered one of our differences. She liked to eat out occasionally while I rarely wanted to. Please let me make clear that she only wanted to dine out occasionally, unlike many spouses who seem to want to eat out four or five times a week. However, her desire to occasionally eat out looked to me like overindulgence. Growing up, my family would go out to eat once a year. Even though the times had changed and, unlike my parents, we had the money to eat out occasionally, I still thought that the correct answer to this issue was to rarely eat out. This had also been an issue in my second marriage, and it was a battle that I often won. But I lost the war. Would I repeat the same mistake again? 2 Corinthians 5:17 says, *"Therefore if anyone is in Christ, he is a new creature; the old things passed away; behold, new things have come."*

Because of the power of God that lives in me, I did not make the same mistake. Through listening to my wife and other godly counsel, I realized that I was wrong. Judy needed a break from preparing most of our meals and she needed to be treated special by me, and to be continually dated. She listened to my story of growing up, and therefore appreciated where I was coming from and understood that eating out a lot was foreign to me. Together, we have found common ground on this financial issue and our marriage is stronger because of the way we reached out to one other. We have cultivated oneness in our marriage by dealing with this issue and others with *"humility and gentleness, with patience, showing tolerance for one another in love"* (Ephesians 4:2).

According to a Barna Group survey, seventy-five percent of Americans say they are Christians, but only twelve percent identify faith as the top priority in their life. This percentage rises to thirty-nine percent among those who consider themselves evangelicals. Faith is outranked by family (forty-five percent); by health, leisure, and a balanced lifestyle (twenty percent); and by wealth, moneymaking, and career success (seventeen percent). Regarding why a lot of American religion is only skin-deep, the president of the Barna Group once pointed to the telling gap between what people prioritize and what they call themselves.

This survey confirms the results of counselees who have come to LifeChange Concepts for one-on-one counseling. We tell the counselees that how well they do in becoming biblical financial stewards depends more on their spiritual maturity than their worldly knowledge and skills. The Apostle Peter wrote, *"Be of sober spirit, be on the alert. Your adversary, the devil, prowls around like a roaring lion, seeking someone to devour. But resist him, firm in your faith…"* (1 Peter 5:8–9) About twenty-five to thirty percent of LCC counselees would list faith and trusting God as a high priority in their lives when they arrive for counseling, or they mature enough during the counseling to be transformed into biblical financial stewards. These families make changes in the way they think and act so that they are aligned with God's Word on money. They have the mind of Christ. As a result, they begin to experience oneness in their finances and marriages.

Everyone who comes to LCC is at a different place in their spiritual walk. We understand this and therefore realize that every counselee isn't going to leave us completely onboard with God's plan for their lives. However, we do rejoice that most counselees leave LCC changed to some degree. My hope is that *Love, Honor, and Finances* has transformed the way you think about managing the money and resources God has entrusted to you, and the way you think about and relate to your spouse. In addition, I hope you will become more purposeful in studying the Bible and becoming a doer of the Word. By implementing many of the biblical truths you have learned here into your marriage and finances, you will win the war.

If this book has helped your marriage, then pass it on to a friend and email me at rlynch6@tamapbay.rr.com to share your success. Godspeed.

Budgeting for the Non-Accountant

A Biblical Perspective of Stewardship

168 pages

$12.95 plus S&H

Available at

www.lifechangeconcepts.org

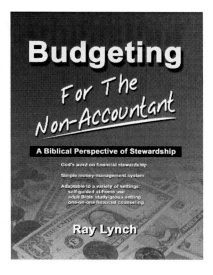

We live in an age of debt. Personal debt is at an all-time high. Student loan debt has surpassed credit card debt. A lifetime of car payments is the norm. All this debt was supposed to make our lives better. Instead, it has brought pain to many in the world. But it doesn't have to be that way. In the **Budgeting for the Non-Accountant** workbook biblical teachings of financial stewardship are combined with a simple and practical budgeting system to enable the reader to break free from the bondage of debt and begin living an abundant life of joy, peace, and contentment.